**PREPARED FOR PUBLICATION
BY
HISTORIC PUBLISHING**

All Rights Reserved. No part of this publication may be reproduced, stored in a retrieval system, or transmitted, in any form, or by any means, electronic, mechanical, photocopying, recording, or otherwise, without the prior consent of the publisher.

**All Rights Reserved
HISTORIC PUBLISHING
©2017**

Narratives of the Sufferings of Lewis and Milton Clarke, Sons of a Soldier of the Revolution, During a Captivity of More Than Twenty Years Among the Slaveholders of Kentucky,
One of the So Called Christian States of North America.
Dictated By Themselves
By

Lewis Garrard Clarke 1812-1897

Milton Clarke 1817-1901

NARRATIVES

OF THE SUFFERINGS OF

LEWIS AND MILTON CLARKE,

SONS OF A SOLDIER OF THE REVOLUTION,

DURING A

CAPTIVITY OF MORE THAN TWENTY YEARS

AMONG THE

SLAVEHOLDERS OF KENTUCKY,

ONE OF THE

SO CALLED CHRISTIAN STATES OF NORTH AMERICA.

DICTATED BY THEMSELVES.

BOSTON:
PUBLISHED BY BELA MARSH,
NO. 25 CORNHILL.
1846.

All Orders to be sent to the Publisher.
PRICE, 25 CENTS.

Entered according to Act of Congress, in the year 1846, by LEWIS AND MILTON CLARKE, in the Clerk's Office of the District Court of the District of Massachusetts.

NARRATIVES OF THE SUFFERINGS OF LEWIS AND MILTON CLARKE, SONS OF A SOLDIER OF THE REVOLUTION, DURING A CAPTIVITY OF MORE THAN TWENTY YEARS AMONG THE SLAVEHOLDERS OF KENTUCKY, ONE OF THE SO CALLED CHRISTIAN STATES OF NORTH AMERICA.

DICTATED BY THEMSELVES.

LARGE PRINT

BOSTON:
PUBLISHED BY BELA MARSH,
NO. 25 CORNHILL.
1846.
All Orders to be sent to the Publisher.

Entered according to Act of Congress, in the year 1846, by LEWIS AND MILTON CLARKE, in the Clerk's Office of the District Court of the District of Massachusetts.

CONTENTS

PREFACE……………………………….16

NARRATIVE OF LEWIS CLARKE………….23

"PROGRESS OF FREEDOM……………………103

NARRATIVE OF MILTON CLARKE…………..114

PREFACE.

I FIRST became acquainted with LEWIS CLARKE in December, 1842. I well remember the deep impression made upon my mind on hearing his Narrative from his own lips. It gave me a new and more vivid impression of the wrongs of Slavery than I had ever before felt. Evidently a person of good native talents and of deep sensibilities, such a mind had been under the dark cloud of slavery for more than twenty-five years. Letters, reading, all the modes of thought awakened by them, had been utterly hid from his eyes; and yet his mind had evidently been active, and trains of thought were flowing through it which he was utterly unable to express. I well remember, too, the wave on wave of deep feeling excited in an audience of more than a thousand persons, at Hallowell, Me., as they listened to his story, and looked upon his energetic and manly countenance, and wondered if the dark cloud of slavery could cover up--hide from the world, and degrade to the condition of brutes--such immortal minds. His story, there and wherever since told, has aroused the most utter abhorrence of the Slave System.

For the last two years, I have had the most ample opportunity of becoming acquainted with Mr. Clarke. He has made this place his home, when not engaged in giving to public audiences the story of his sufferings and the sufferings of his fellow-slaves. Soon after he came to Ohio, by the faithful instruction of pious friends, he was led, as he believes, to see himself a sinner before God, and to seek pardon and forgiveness through the precious blood of the Lamb. He has ever manifested an ardent thirst for religious, as well as for other hinds of knowledge. In the opinion of all those best acquainted with him, he has maintained the character of a sincere Christian. That he is what he professes to be,--a slave escaped from the grasp of avarice and power,--there is not the least shadow of doubt. His Narrative bears the most conclusive internal evidence of its truth. Persons of discriminating minds have heard it repeatedly, under a great variety of circumstances, and the story, in all substantial respects, has been always the same. He has been repeatedly recognized in the Free States, by persons who knew him in Kentucky, when a slave. During the summer of 1844, Cassius M. Clay visited Boston, and, on seeing Milton Clarke, recognized him as one of the Clarke family, well known to him in Kentucky. Indeed, nothing can be more surely established than the fact that Lewis and Milton Clarke are no impostors. For three years they have been engaged in telling their story in seven or eight different states, and no one has appeared to make an attempt to contradict them. The capture of Milton in Ohio, by the kidnappers, as a slave, makes assurance doubly strong. Wherever they have told their story, large audiences have collected, and every where they have been listened to with great interest and satisfaction.

Cyrus is fully equal to either of the brothers in sprightliness of mind--is withal a great wit, and would make an admirable lecturer, but for an unfortunate impediment in his speech. They all feel deeply the wrongs they have suffered, and are by no means forgetful of their brethren in bonds. When Lewis first came to this place, he was frequently noticed in silent and deep meditation. On being asked what he was thinking of, he would reply, "O, of the poor slaves! Here I am free, and they suffering so much." Bitter tears are often seen coursing down his manly checks, as he recurs to the scenes of his early suffering. Many persons, who have heard him lecture, have expressed a strong desire that his story might be recorded in a collected form. He has, therefore, concluded to have it printed. He was anxious to spread the story of his sufferings as extensively as possible before the community, that he might awaken more hearts to feel for his down-trodden brethren. Nothing seems to grieve him to the heart, like finding a minister of the gospel, or a professed Christian, indifferent to the condition of the slave. As to doing much for the instruction of the minds of the slaves, or for the salvation of their souls, till they are

EMANCIPATED, restored to the rights of men, in his opinion it is utterly impossible.

When the master, or his representative, the man who justifies slaveholding, comes with the whip in one hand and the Bible in the other, the slave says, at least in his heart, Lay down one or the other. Either make the tree good and the fruit good, or else both corrupt together. Slaves do not believe that THE RELIGION which is from God, bears whips and chains. They ask, emphatically, concerning their FATHER in heaven,

"Has HE bid you buy and sell us;
Speaking from his throne, the sky?"

For the facts contained in the following Narrative, Mr. Clarke is of course alone responsible. Yet, having had the most ample opportunities for testing his accuracy, I do not hesitate to say, that I have not a shadow of doubt but in all material points every word is true. Much of it is in his own language, and all of it according to his own dictation.

J. C. LOVEJOY.

CAMBRIDGEPORT, April, 1845.

NARRATIVE OF LEWIS CLARKE.

NARRATIVE OF LEWIS CLARKE.

I WAS born in March, as near as I can ascertain, in the year 1815, in Madison county, Kentucky, about seven miles from Richmond, upon the plantation of my grandfather, Samuel Campbell. He was considered a very respectable man, among his fellow-robbers, the slaveholders. It did not render him less honorable in their eyes that he took to his bed Mary, his slave, perhaps half white, by whom he had one daughter, LETITIA CAMPBELL. This was before his marriage.

My father was from "beyond the flood"--from Scotland, and by trade a weaver. He had been married in his own country, and lost his wife, who left to him, as I have been told, two sons. He came to this country in time to be in the earliest scenes of the American revolution. He was at the battle of Bunker Hill, and continued in the army to the close of the war. About the year 1800, or before, he came to Kentucky, and married Miss Letitia Campbell, then held as a slave by her dear and affectionate father. My father died, as near as I can recollect, when I was about ten or twelve years of age. He had received a wound in the war, which made him lame as long as he lived. I have often heard him tell of Scotland, sing the merry songs of his native land, and long to see its hills once more.

Mr. Campbell promised my father that his daughter Letitia should be made free in his will. It was with this promise that he married her. And I have no doubt that Mr. Campbell was as good as his word, and that, by his will, my mother and her nine children were made free. But ten persons in one family, each worth three hundred dollars, are not easily set free among those accustomed to live by continued robbery. We did not, therefore, by an instrument from the hand of the dead, escape the avaricious grab of the slaveholder. It is the common belief that the will was destroyed by the heirs of Mr. Campbell.

The night in which I was born, I have been told, was dark and terrible--black as the night for which Job prayed, when he besought the clouds to pitch their tent round about the place of his birth; and my life of slavery was but too exactly prefigured by the stormy elements that hovered over the first hour of my being. It was with great difficulty that any one could be urged out for a necessary attendant for my mother. At length, one of the sons of Mr. Campbell, William, by the promise from his mother of the child that should be born, was induced to make an effort to obtain the necessary assistance. By going five or six miles, he obtained a female professor of the couch.

William Campbell, by virtue of this title, always claimed me as his property. And well would it have been for me if this claim had been regarded. At the age of six or seven years, I fell into the hands of his sister, Mrs. Betsey Banton, whose character will be best known when I have told the horrid wrongs which she heaped upon me for ten years. If there are any she spirits that come up front hell, and take possession of one part of mankind, I am sure she is one of that sort. I was consigned to her under the following circumstances: When she was married, there was given her, as part of her dower, as is common among the Algerines of Kentucky, a girl, by the name of Ruth, about fourteen or fifteen years old. In a short time, Ruth was dejected and injured, by beating and abuse of different kinds, so that she was sold, for a half-fool, to the more tender mercies of the sugar-planter in Louisiana. The amiable Mrs. Betsey obtained then, on loan from her parents, another slave, named Phillis. In six months she had suffered so severely, under the hand of this monster-woman, that she made an attempt to kill herself, and was taken home by the parents of Mrs. Banton. This produced a regular slaveholding family brawl; a regular war, of four years, between the mild and peaceable Mrs. B. and her own parents. These wars are very common among the Algerines in Kentucky; indeed, slaveholders have not arrived at that degree of civilization that enables them to live in tolerable peace, though united by the nearest family ties. In them is fulfilled what I have heard read in the Bible-- "The father is against the son, and the daughter-in-law against the mother-in-law, and their foes are of their own household." Some of the slaveholders may have a wide house; but one of the cat-handed, snake-eyed, brawling women, which slavery produces, can fill it from cellar to garret. I have heard every place I could get into any way ring with their screech-owl voices. Of all the animals on the face of this earth, I am most afraid of a real mad, passionate, raving, slaveholding woman. Somebody told me, once, that Edmund Burke declared that the natives of India fled to the jungles, among tigers and lions, to escape the more barbarous cruelty of Warren Hastings. I am sure I would sooner lie down to sleep by the side of tigers than near a raging-mad slave woman. But I must go back to sweet Mrs. Banton. I have been describing her in the abstract. I will give a full-grown portrait of her right away. For four years after the trouble about Phillis she never came near her father's house. At the end of this period, another of the amiable sisters was to be married, and sister Betsey could not repress the tide of curiosity urging her to be present at the nuptial ceremonies. Beside, she had another motive. Either shrewdly suspecting that she might deserve less than any member of the family, or that some ungrounded partiality would be manifested toward her sister, she determined, at all hazards, to be present, and see that the scales which weighed out the children of the plantation should be held with even hand. The wedding-day was appointed; the sons and daughters of this joyful occasion were gathered together, and then came also the fair-faced, but black-hearted, Mrs. B. Satan, among the sons of God, was never less welcome than this fury among her kindred. They all knew what she came for,--to make mischief, if possible. "Well, now, if there aint Bets!" exclaimed the old lady. The father was moody and silent, knowing that she inherited largely of the disposition of her mother; but he had experienced too many of her retorts of courtesy to say as much, for dear experience had taught him the discretion of silence. The brothers smiled at the prospect of fun and frolic; the sisters trembled for fear, and word flew round among the slaves, "The old she-bear has come home! look out! look out!"

The wedding went forward. Polly, a very good sort of a girl to be raised in that region, was married, and received, as the first instalment of her dower, a girl and a boy. Now was the time for Mrs. Banton, sweet, good Mrs. Banton. "Poll has a girl and a boy, and I only had that fool of a girl. I reckon, if I go home without a boy too, this house won't be left standing."

This was said, too, while the sugar of the wedding-cake was yet melting upon her tongue. How the bitter words would flow when the guests had retired, all began to imagine. To arrest this whirlwind of rising passion, her mother promised any boy upon the plantation, to be taken home on her return. Now, my evil star was right in the top of the sky. Every boy was ordered in, to pass before this female sorceress, that she might select a victim for her unprovoked malice, and on whom to pour the vials of her wrath for years. I was that unlucky fellow. Mr. Campbell, my grandfather, objected, because it would divide a family, and offered her Moses, whose father and mother had been sold south. Mrs. Campbell put in for William's claim, dated ante natum--before I was born; but objections and claims of every kind were swept away by the wild passion and shrill-toned voice of Mrs. B. Me she would have, and none else. Mr. Campbell went out to hunt, and drive away bad thoughts; the old lady became quiet, for she was sure none of her blood run in my veins, and, if there was any of her husband's there, it was no fault of hers. Slave women are always revengeful toward the children of slaves that have any of the blood of their husbands in them. I was too young, only seven years of age, to understand what was going on. But my poor and affectionate mother understood and appreciated it all. When she left the kitchen of the mansion-house, where she was employed as cook, and came home to her own little cottage, the tear of anguish was in her eye, and the image of sorrow upon every feature of her face. She knew the female Nero, whose rod was now to be over me. That night sleep departed from her eyes. With the youngest child clasped firmly to her bosom, she spent the night in walking the floor, coming ever and anon to lift up the clothes and look at me and my poor brother, who lay sleeping together. Sleeping, I said. Brother slept, but not I. I saw my mother when she first came to me, and I could not sleep. The vision of that night--its deep, ineffaceable impression--is now before my mind with all the distinctness of yesterday. In the morning, I was put into the carriage with Mrs. B. and her children, and my weary pilgrimage of suffering was fairly begun. It was her business on the road, for about twenty-five or thirty miles, to initiate her children into the art of tormenting their new victim. I was seated upon the bottom of the carriage, and these little imps were employed in pinching me, pulling my ears and hair; and they were stirred up by their mother, like a litter of young wolves, to torment me in every way possible. In the mean time, I was compelled by the old she-wolf to call them "Master," "Mistress," and bow to them, and obey them at the first call.

During that day, I had, indeed, no very agreeable foreboding of the torments to come; but, sad as were my anticipations, the reality was infinitely beyond them. Infinitely more bitter than death were the cruelties I experienced at the hand of this merciless woman. Save from one or two slaves on the plantation, during my ten years of captivity here, I scarcely heard a kind word, or saw a smile toward me from any living being. And now that I am where people look kind, and act kindly toward me, it seems like a dream. I hardly seem to be in the same world that I was then. When I first got into the free states, and saw everybody look like they loved one another, sure enough, I thought, this must be the "Heaven" of LOVE I had heard something about. But I must go back to what I suffered from that wicked woman. It is hard work to keep the mind upon it; I hate to think it over--but I must tell it--the world must know what is done in Kentucky. I cannot, however, tell all the ways by which she tormented me. I can only give a few instances of my suffering, as specimens of the whole. A book of a thousand pages would not be large enough to tell of all the tears I shed, and the sufferings endured, in THAT TEN YEARS OF PURGATORY.

A very trivial offence was sufficient to call forth a great burst of indignation from this woman of ungoverned passions. In my simplicity, I put my lips to the same vessel, and drank out of it, from which her children were accustomed to drink. She expressed her utter abhorrence of such an act, by throwing my head violently back, and dashing into my face two dippers of water. The shower of water was followed by a heavier shower of kicks; yes, delicate reader, this lady did not hesitate to kick, as well as cuff in a very plentiful manner; but the words, bitter and cutting, that followed, were like a storm of hail upon my young heart. "She would teach me better manners than that; she would let me know I was to be brought up to her hand; she would have one slave that knew his place; if I wanted water, go to the spring, and not drink there in the house." This was new times for me; for some days I was completely benumbed with my sorrow. I could neither eat nor sleep. If there is any human being on earth, who has been so blessed as never to have tasted the cup of sorrow, and therefore is unable to conceive of suffering; if there be one so lost to all feeling as even to say, that the slaves do not suffer when families are separated, let such a one go to the ragged quilt which was my couch and pillow, and stand there night after night, for long, weary hours, and see the bitter tears streaming down the face of that more than orphan boy, while, with half-suppressed sighs and sobs, he calls again and again upon his absent mother.

"Say, mother, wast thou conscious of the tears I shed?
Hovered thy spirit o'er thy sorrowing son?
Wretch even then! life's journey just begun."

Let him stand by that couch of bitter sorrow

through the terribly lonely night, and then wring out the wet end of those rags, and see how many tears yet remain, after the burning temples had absorbed all they could. He will not doubt, he cannot doubt, but the slave has feeling. But I find myself running away again from Mrs. Banton--and I don't much wonder neither.

There were several children in the family, and my first main business was to wait upon them. Another young slave and myself have often been compelled to sit up by turns all night, to rock the cradle of a little, peevish scion of slavery. If the cradle was stopped, the moment they awoke a dolorous cry was sent forth to mother or father, that Lewis had gone to sleep. The reply to this call would be a direction from the mother for these petty tyrants to get up and take the whip, and give the good-for-nothing scoundrel a smart whipping. This was the midnight pastime of a child ten or twelve years old. What might you expect of the future man?

There were four house-slaves in this family, including myself; and though we had not, in all respects, so hard work as the field hands, yet in many things our condition was much worse. We were constantly exposed to the whims and passions of every member of the family; from the least to the greatest, their anger was wreaked upon us. Nor was our life an easy one, in the hours of our toil or in the amount of labor performed. We were always required to sit up until all the family had retired; then we must be up at early dawn in summer, and before day in winter. If we failed, through weariness or for any other reason, to appear at the first morning summons, we were sure to have our hearing quickened by a severe chastisement. Such horror has seized me, lest I might not hear the first shrill call, that I have often in dreams fancied I heard that unwelcome voice, and have leaped from my couch, and walked through the house and out of it before I awoke. I have gone and called the other slaves, in my sleep, and asked them if they did not hear master call. Never, while I live, will the remembrance of those long, bitter nights of fear pass from my mind.

But I want to give you a few specimens of the abuse which I received. During the ten years that I lived with Mrs. Banton, I do not think there were as many days, when she was at home, that I, or some other slave, did not receive some kind of beating or abuse at her hands. It seemed as though she could not live nor sleep unless some poor back was smarting, some head beating with pain, or some eye filled with tears around her. Her tender mercies were indeed cruel. She brought up her children to imitate her example. Two of them manifested some dislike to the cruelties taught them by their mother, but they never stood high in favor with her; indeed, anything like humanity or kindness to a slave, was looked upon by her as a great offence.

Her instruments of torture were ordinarily the raw hide, or a bunch of hickory-sprouts seasoned in the fire and tied together. But if these were not at hand, nothing came amiss. She could relish a beating with a chair, the broom, tongs, shovel, shears, knife-handle, the heavy heel of her slipper, or a bunch of keys; her zeal was so active in these barbarous inflictions, that her invention was wonderfully quick, and some way of inflicting the requisite torture was soon found out.

One instrument of torture is worthy of particular description This was an oak club, a foot and a half in length and an inch and a half square. With this delicate weapon she would beat us upon the hands and upon the feet until they were blistered. This instrument was carefully preserved for a period of four years. Every day, for that time, I was compelled to see that hated tool of cruelty lying in the chair by my side. The least degree of delinquency either in not doing all the appointed work, or in look or behavior, was visited with a beating from this oak club. That club will always be a prominent object in the picture of horrors of my life of more than twenty years of bitter bondage.

When about nine years old, I was sent in the evening to catch and kill a turkey. They were securely sleeping in a tree--their accustomed resting-place for the night. I approached as cautiously as possible, and selected the victim I was directed to catch; but, just as I grasped him in my hand, my foot slipped, and he made his escape from the tree, and fled beyond my reach. I returned with a heavy heart to my mistress with the story of my misfortune. She was enraged beyond measure. She determined, at once, that I should have a whipping of the worst kind, and she was bent upon adding all the aggravations possible. Master had gone to bed drunk, and was now as fast asleep as drunkards ever are. At any rate, he was filling the house with the noise of his snoring and with the perfume of his breath. I was ordered to go and call him--wake him up-- and ask him to be kind enough to give me fifty good smart lashes. To be whipped is bad enough--to ask for it is worse--to ask a drunken man to whip you is too bad. I would sooner have gone to a nest of rattlesnakes, than to the bed of this drunkard. But go I must. Softly I crept along, and gently shaking his arm, said, with a trembling voice, "Master, master, mistress wants you to wake up." This did not go to the extent of her command, and in a great fury she called out, "What, you wont ask him to whip you, will you?" I then added, "Mistress wants you to give me fifty lashes." A bear at the smell of a lamb was never roused quicker. "Yes, yes, that I will; I'll give you such a whipping as you will never want again." And, sure enough, so he did. He sprang from the bed, seized me by the hair, lashed me with a handful of switches, threw me my whole length upon the floor; beat, kicked, and cuffed me worse than he would a dog, and then threw me, with all his strength, out of the door, more dead than alive. There I lay for a long time, scarcely able and not daring to move, till I could bear no sound of the furies within, and then crept to my couch, longing for death to put an end to my misery. I had no friend in the world to whom I could utter one word of complaint, or to whom I could look for protection.

Mr. Banton owned a blacksmith's shop, in which he spent some of his time, though he was not a very efficient hand at the forge. One day, mistress told me to go over to the shop and let master give me a flogging. I knew the mode of punishing there too well. I would rather die than go. The poor fellow who worked in the shop, a very skilful workman, one day came to the determination that he would work no more, unless he could be paid for his labor. The enraged master put a handful of nail-rods into the fire, and when they were red-hot, took them out, and cooled one after another of them in the blood and flesh of the poor slave's back. I knew this was the shop mode of punishment. I would not go; and Mr. Banton came home, and his amiable lady told him the story of my refusal. He broke forth in a great rage, and gave me a most unmerciful beating; adding that, if I had come, he would have burned the hot nail-rods into my back.

Mrs. Banton, as is common among slaveholding women, seemed to hate and abuse me all the more, because I had some of the blood of her father in my veins. There are no slaves that are so badly abused, as those that are related to some of the women, or the children of their own husband; it seems as though they never could hate these quite bad enough. My sisters were as white and good-looking as any of the young ladies in Kentucky. It happened once of a time, that a young man called at the house of Mr. Campbell, to see a sister of Mrs. Banton. Seeing one of my sisters in the house, and pretty well dressed, with a strong family look, he thought it was Miss Campbell; and, with that supposition, addressed some conversation to her, which he had intended for the private car of Miss C. The mistake was noised abroad, and occasioned some amusement to young people. Mrs. Banton heard of it, and it made her caldron of wrath sizzling hot; everything that diverted and amused other people seemed to enrage her. There are hot-springs in Kentucky; she was just like one of them, only brimful of boiling poison.

She must wreak her vengeance, for this innocent mistake of the young man, upon me. "She would fix me, so that nobody should ever think I was white." Accordingly, in a burning hot day, she made me take off every rag of clothes, go out into the garden, and pick herbs for hours, in order to burn me black. When I went out, she threw cold water on me, so that the sun might take effect upon me; when I came in, she gave me a severe beating on my blistered back.

After I had lived with Mrs. B. three or four years, I was put to spinning hemp, flax, and tow, on an old-fashioned foot-wheel. There were four or five slaves at this business, a good part of the time. We were kept at our work from daylight to dark in summer, from long before day to nine or ten o'clock in the evening in winter. Mrs. Banton, for the most part, was near, or kept continually passing in and out, to see that each of us performed as much work as she thought we ought to do. Being young, and sick at heart all the time, it was very hard work to go through the day and evening and not suffer exceedingly for want of more sleep. Very often, too, I was compelled to work beyond the ordinary hour, to finish the appointed task of the day. Sometimes I found it impossible not to drop asleep at the wheel.

On these occasions, Mrs. B. had her peculiar contrivances for keeping us awake. She would sometimes sit, by the hour, with a dipper of vinegar and salt, and throw it in my eyes to keep them open. My hair was pulled till there was no longer any pain from that source. And I can now suffer myself to be lifted by the hair of the head, without experiencing the least pain.

She very often kept me from getting water to satisfy my thirst, and in one instance kept me for two entire days without a particle of food. This she did, in order that I might make up for lost time. But, of course, I lost rather than gained upon my task. Every meal taken from me made me less able to work. It finally ended in a terrible beating.

But all my severe labor, and bitter and cruel punishments, for these ten years of captivity with this worse than Arab family, all these were as nothing to the sufferings I experienced by being separated from my mother, brothers, and sisters; the same things, with them near to sympathize with me, to hear my story of sorrow, would have been comparatively tolerable.

They were distant only about thirty miles; and yet, in ten long, lonely years of childhood, I was only permitted to see them three times.

My mother occasionally found an opportunity to send me some token of remembrance and affection, a sugar-plum or an apple; but I scarcely ever ate them; they were laid up, and handled and wept over till they wasted away in my hand.

My thoughts continually by day, and my dreams by night, were of mother and home; and the horror experienced in the morning, when I awoke and behold it was a dream, is beyond the power of language to describe.

But I am about to leave this den of robbers, where I had been so long imprisoned. I cannot, however, call the reader from his new and pleasant acquaintance with this amiable pair, without giving a few more incidents of their history. When this is done, and I have taken great pains, as I shall do, to put a copy of this portrait in the hands of this Mrs. B., I shall bid her farewell. If she sees something awfully hideous in her picture, as here presented, she will be constrained to acknowledge it is true to nature. I have given it from no malice, no feeling of resentment towards her, but that the world may know what is done by slavery, and that slaveholders may know that their crimes will come to light. I hope and pray that Mrs. B. will repent of her many and aggravated sins before it is too late.

The scenes between her and her husband, while I was with them, strongly illustrate the remark of Jefferson, that slavery fosters the worst passions of the master. Scarcely a day passed, in which bitter words were not bandied from one to the other. I have seen Mrs. B., with a large knife drawn in her right hand, the other upon the collar of her husband, swearing and threatening to cut him square in two. They both drank freely, and swore like highwaymen. He was a gambler and a counterfeiter. I have seen and handled his moulds and his false coin. They finally quarrelled openly, and separated; and the last I knew of them, he was living a sort of poor vagabond life in his native state, and she was engaged in a protracted lawsuit with some of her former friends, about her father's property.

Of course, such habits did not produce great thrift in their worldly condition, and myself and other slaves were mortgaged, from time to time, to make up the deficiency between their income and expenses. I was transferred, at the age of sixteen or seventeen, to a Mr. K., whose name I forbear to mention, lest, if he or any other man should ever claim property where they never had any, this, my own testimony, might be brought in to aid their wicked purposes.

In the exchange of masters, my condition was, in many respects, greatly improved. I was free, at any rate, from that kind of suffering experienced at the hand of Mrs. B., as though she delighted in cruelty for its own sake. My situation, however, with Mr. K. was far from enviable. Taken from the work in and around the house, and put at once, at that early age, to the constant work of a full-grown man, I found it not an easy task always to escape the lash of the overseer. In the four or five years that I was with this man, the overseers were often changed. Sometimes we had a man that seemed to have some consideration, some mercy; but generally their eye seemed to be fixed upon one object, and that was, to get the greatest possible amount of work out of every slave upon the plantation. When stooping to clear the tobacco-plants from the worms which infest them, --a work which draws most cruelly upon the back, --some of these men would not allow us a moment to rest at the end of the row; but, at the crack of the whip, we were compelled to jump to our places, from row to row, for hours, while the poor back was crying out with torture. Any complaint or remonstrance under such circumstances is sure to be answered in no other way than by the lash. As a sheep before her shearers is dumb, so a slave is not permitted to open his mouth.

There were about one hundred and fifteen slaves upon this plantation. Generally, we had enough, in quantity, of food. We had, however, but two meals a day, of corn-meal bread and soup, or meat of the poorest kind. Very often, so little care had been taken to cure and preserve the bacon, that, when it came to us, though it had been fairly killed once, it was more alive than dead. Occasionally, we had some refreshment over and above the two meals, but this was extra, beyond the rules of the plantation. And, to balance this gratuity, we were also frequently deprived of our food, as a punishment. We suffered greatly, too, for want of water. The slave-drivers have the notion that slaves are more healthy, if allowed to drink but little, than they are if freely allowed nature's beverage. The slaves quite as confidently cherish the opinion that, if the master would drink less peach brandy and whisky, and give the slave more water, it would be better all round. As it is, the more the master and overseer drink, the less they seem to think the slave needs.

In the winter, we took our meals before day in the morning, and after work at night; in the summer, at about nine o'clock in the morning, and at two in the afternoon. When we were cheated out of our two meals a day, either by the cruelty or caprice of the overseer, we always felt it a kind of special duty and privilege to make up, in some way, the deficiency. To accomplish this, we had many devices; and we sometimes resorted to our peculiar methods, when incited only by a desire to taste greater variety than our ordinary bill of fare afforded.

This sometimes led to very disastrous results. The poor slave who was caught with a chicken or a pig, killed from the plantation, had his back scored most unmercifully. Nevertheless, the pigs would die without being sick or squealing once; and the hens, chickens, and turkeys sometimes disappeared, and never stuck up a feather to tell where they were buried. The old goose would sometimes exchange her whole nest of eggs for round pebbles; and, patient as that animal is, this quality was exhausted, and she was obliged to leave her nest with no train of offspring behind her.

One old slave woman upon this plantation was altogether too keen and shrewd for the best of them. She would go out to the corn-crib with her basket, watch her opportunity, with one effective blow pop over a little pig, slip him into her basket, and put the cobs on top, trudge off to her cabin, and look just as innocent as though she had a right to eat of the work of her own hands. It was a kind of first principle, too, in her code of morals, that they that worked had a right to eat. The moral of all questions in relation to taking food was easily settled by aunt Peggy. The only question with her was, how arid when to do it.

It could not be done openly, that was plain. It must be done secretly; if not in the daytime, by all means in the night. With a dead pig in the cabin, and the water all hot for scalding, she was at one time warned by her son that the Philistines were upon her. Her resources were fully equal to the sudden emergency. Quick as thought, the pig was thrown into the boiling kettle, a door was put over it, her daughter seated upon it, and, with a good, thick quilt around her, the overseer found little Clara taking a steam-bath for a terrible cold. The daughter, acting well her part, groaned sadly; the mother was very busy in tucking in the quilt, and the overseer was blinded, and went away without seeing a bristle of the pig.

Aunt P. cooked for herself, for another slave named George, and for me. George was very successful in bringing home his share of the plunder. He could capture a pig or a turkey without exciting the least suspicion. The old lady often rallied me for want of courage for such enterprises. At length, I summoned resolution, one rainy night, and determined there should be one from the herd of swine brought home by my hands. I went to the crib of corn, got my ear to shell, and my cart-stake to despatch a little roaster. I raised my arm to strike, summoned courage again and again, but to no purpose. The scattered kernels were all picked up, and no blow struck. Again I visited the crib, selected my victim, and struck! The blow glanced upon the side of the head, and, instead of falling, he ran off, squealing louder than ever I heard a pig squeal before. I ran as fast, in an opposite direction, made a large circuit, and reached the cabin, emptied the hot water, and made for my couch as soon as possible. I escaped detection, and only suffered from the ridicule of old Peggy and young George.

Poor Jess, upon the same plantation, did not so easily escape. More successful in his effort, he killed his pig; but he was found out. He was hung up by the hands, with a rail between his feet, and full three hundred lashes scored in upon his naked back. For a long time his life hung in doubt; and his poor wife, for becoming a partaker after the fact, was most severely beaten.

Another slave, employed as a driver upon the plantation, was compelled to whip his own wife, for a similar offence, so severely that she never recovered from the cruelty. She was literally whipped to death by her own husband.

A slave, called Hall, the hostler on the plantation, made a successful sally, one night, upon the animals forbidden to the Jews. The next day, he went into the barn-loft, and fell asleep. While sleeping over his abundant supper, and dreaming, perhaps, of his feast, he heard the shrill voice of his master, crying out, "The hogs are at the horse-trough; where is Hall?" The "hogs" and "Hall," coupled together, were enough for the poor fellow. He sprung from the hay, and made the best of his way off the plantation. He was gone six months; and, at the end of this period, he procured the intercession of the son-in-law of his master, and returned, escaping the ordinary punishment. But the transgression was laid up. Slaveholders seldom forgive; they only postpone the time of revenge. When about to be severely flogged, for some pretended offence, he took two of his grandsons, and escaped as far towards Canada as Indiana. He was followed, captured, brought back, and whipped most horribly. All the old score had been treasured up against him, and his poor back atoned for the whole at once.

On this plantation was a slave, named Sam, whose wife lived a few miles distant; and Sam was very seldom permitted to go and see his family. He worked in the blacksmith's shop. For a small offence, he was hung up by the hands, a rail between his feet, and whipped in turn by the master, overseer, and one of the waiters, till his back was torn all to pieces; and, in less than two months, Sam was in his grave. His last words were, "Mother, tell master he has killed me at last, for nothing; but tell him if God will forgive him I will."

A very poor white woman lived within about a mile of the plantation house. A female slave, named Flora, knowing she was in a very suffering condition, shelled out a peck of corn, and carried it to her in the night. Next day, the old man found it out, and this deed of charity was atoned for by one hundred and fifty lashes upon the bare back of poor Flora.

The master with whom I now lived was a very passionate man. At one time he thought the work on the plantation did not go on as it ought. One morning, when he and the overseer waked up from a drunken frolic, they swore the hands should not eat a morsel of anything, till a field of wheat of some sixty acres was all cradled. There were from thirty to forty hands to do the work. We were driven on to the extent of our strength, and, although a brook ran through the field, not one of us was permitted to stop and taste a drop of water. Some of the men were so exhausted that they reeled for very weakness; two of the women fainted, and one of them was severely whipped, to revive her. They were at last carried helpless from the field and thrown down under the shade of a tree. At about five o'clock in the afternoon the wheat was all cut, and we were permitted to eat. Our suffering for want of water was excruciating. I trembled all over from the inward gnawing of hunger and from burning thirst.

In view of the sufferings of this day, we felt fully justified in making a foraging expedition upon the milk-room that night. And when master, and overseer, and all hands were locked up in sleep, ten or twelve of us went down to the spring house; a house built over a spring, to keep the milk and other things cool. We pressed altogether against the door, and open it came. We found half of a good baked pig, plenty of cream, milk, and other delicacies; and, as we felt in some measure delegated to represent all that had been cheated of their meals the day before, we ate plentifully. But after a successful plundering expedition within the gates of the enemy's camp, it is not easy always to cover the retreat. We had a reserve in the pasture for this purpose. We went up to the herd of swine, and, with a milk-pail in hand, it was easy to persuade them there was more where that came from, and the whole tribe followed readily into the spring house, and we left them there to wash the dishes and wipe up the floor, while we retired to rest. This was not malice in us; we did not love the waste which the hogs made; but we must have something to eat, to pay for the cruel and reluctant fast; and when we had obtained this, we must of course cover up our track. They watch us narrowly; and to take an egg, a pound of meat, or anything else, however hungry we may be, is considered a great crime; we are compelled, therefore, to waste a good deal sometimes, to get a little.

I lived with this Mr. K. about four or five years; I then fell into the hands of his son. He was a drinking, ignorant man, but not so cruel as his father. Of him I hired my time at $12 a month; boarded and clothed myself. To meet my payments, I split rails, burned coal, peddled grass seed, and took hold of whatever I could find to do. This last master, or owner, as he would call himself, died about one year before I left Kentucky. By the administrators I was hired out for a time, and at last put up upon the auction block, for sale. No bid could be obtained for me. There were two reasons in the way. One was, there were two or three old mortgages which were not settled, and the second reason given by the bidders was, I had had too many privileges; had been permitted to trade for myself and go over the state; in short, to use their phrase, I was a "spoilt nigger." And sure enough I was, for all their purposes. I had long thought and dreamed of LIBERTY; I was now determined to make an effort, to gain it. No tongue can tell the doubt, the perplexities, the anxiety which a slave feels, when making up his mind upon this subject. If he makes an effort, and is not successful, he must be laughed at by his fellows; he will be beaten unmercifully by the master, and then watched and used the harder for it all his life.

And then, if he gets away, who, what will he find? He is ignorant of the world. All the white part of mankind, that he has ever seen, are enemies to him and all his kindred. How can he venture where none but white faces shall greet him? The master tells him, that abolitionists decoy slaves off into the free states, to catch them and sell them to Louisiana or Mississippi; and if he goes to Canada, the British will put him in a mine under ground, with both eyes put out, for life. How does he know what, or whom, to believe? A horror of great darkness comes upon him, as he thinks over what may befall him. Long, very long time did I think of escaping before I made the effort.

At length, the report was started that I was to be sold for Louisiana. Then I thought it was time to act. My mind was made up. This was about two weeks before I started. The first plan was formed between a slave named Isaac and myself. Isaac proposed to take one of the horses of his mistress, and I was to take my pony, and we were to ride off together; I as master, and he as slave. We started together, and went on five miles. My want of confidence in the plan induced me to turn back. Poor Isaac plead like a good fellow to go forward. I am satisfied from experience and observation that both of us must have been captured and carried back. I did not know enough at that time to travel and manage a waiter. Everything would have been done in such an awkward manner that a keen eye would have seen through our plot at once. I did not know the roads, and could not have read the guide-boards; and ignorant as many people are in Kentucky, they would have thought it strange to see a man with a waiter, who could not read a guide-board. I was sorry to leave Isaac, but I am satisfied I could have done him no good in the way proposed.

After this failure, I staid about two weeks; and after having arranged everything to the best of my knowledge, I saddled my pony, went into the cellar where I kept my grass-seed apparatus, put my clothes into a pair of saddle-bags, and them into my seed-bag, and, thus equipped, set sail for the north star. O what a day was that to me! This was on Saturday, in August, 1841. I wore my common clothes, and was very careful to avoid special suspicion, as I already imagined the administrator was very watchful of me. The place from which I started was about fifty miles from Lexington. The reason why I do not give the name of the place, and a more accurate location, must be obvious to any one who remembers that, in the eye of the law, I am yet accounted a slave, and no spot in the United States affords an asylum for the wanderer. True, I feel protected in the hearts of the many warm friends of the slave by whom I am surrounded; but this protection does not come from the LAWS of any one of the United States.

But to return. After riding about fifteen miles, a Baptist minister overtook me on the road, saying, "How do you do, boy? are you free? I always thought you were free, till I saw them try to sell you the other day." I then wished him a thousand miles off, preaching, if he would, to the whole plantation, "Servants, obey your masters;" but I wanted neither sermons, questions, nor advice from him. At length I mustered resolution to make some kind of a reply. "What made you think I was free?" He replied, that he had noticed I had great privileges, that I did much as I liked, and that I was almost white. "O yes," I said, "but there are a great many slaves as white as I am." "Yes," he said, and then went on to name several; among others, one who had lately, as he said, run away. This was touching altogether too near upon what I was thinking of. Now, said I, he must know, or at least reckons, what I am at--running away.

However, I blushed as little as possible, and made strange of the fellow who had lately run away, as though I knew nothing of it. The old fellow looked at me, as it seemed to me, as though he would read my thoughts. I wondered what in the world slaves could run away for, especially if they had such a chance as I had had for the last few years. He said, "I suppose you would not run away on any account, you are so well treated." "O," said I, "I do very well, very well, sir. If you should ever hear that I had run away, be certain it must be because there is some great change in my treatment."

He then began to talk with me about the seed in my bag, and said that he should want to buy some. Then, I thought, he means to get at the truth by looking in my seed bag, where, sure enough, he would not find grass seed, but the seeds of Liberty. However, he dodged off soon, and left me alone. And although I have heard say, poor company is better than none, I felt much better without him than with him.

When I had gone on about twenty-five miles, I went down into a deep valley by the side of the road, and changed my clothes. I reached Lexington about seven o'clock that evening, and put up with brother Cyrus. As I had often been to Lexington before, and stopped with him, it excited no attention from the slaveholding gentry. Moreover, I had a pass from the administrator, of whom I had hired my time. I remained over the Sabbath with Cyrus, and we talked over a great many plans for future operations, if my efforts to escape should be successful. Indeed, we talked over all sorts of ways for me to proceed. But both of us were very ignorant of the roads, and of the best way to escape suspicion. And I sometimes wonder that a slave, so ignorant, so timid, as he is, ever makes the attempt to get his freedom. "Without are foes, within are fears."

Monday morning, bright and early, I set my face in good earnest toward the Ohio River, determined to see and tread the north bank of it, or die in the attempt. I said to myself, One of two things,-- FREEDOM OR DEATH! The first night I reached Mayslick, fifty odd miles from Lexington. Just before reaching this village, I stopped to think over my situation, and determine how I would pass that night. On that night hung all my hopes. I was within twenty miles of Ohio. My horse was unable to reach the river that night. And besides, to travel and attempt to cross the river in the night, would excite suspicion. I must spend the night there. But how? At one time, I thought, I will take my pony out into the field and give him some corn, and sleep myself on the grass. But then the dogs will be out in the evening, and, if caught under such circumstances, they will take me for a thief if not for a runaway. That will not do. So, after weighing the matter all over, I made a plunge right into the heart of the village, and put up at the tavern.

After seeing my pony disposed of, I looked into the bar-room, and saw some persons that I thought were from my part of the country, and would know me. I shrunk back with horror. What to do I did not know. I looked across the street, and saw the shop of a silversmith. A thought of a pair of spectacles, to hide my face, struck me. I went across the way, and began to barter for a pair of double-eyed green spectacles. When I got them on, they blind-folded me, if they did not others. Every thing seemed right up in my eyes. Some people buy spectacles to see out of; I bought mine to keep from being seen. I hobbled back to the tavern, and called for supper. This I did to avoid notice, for I felt like anything but eating. At tea, I had not learned to measure distances with my new eyes, and the first pass I made with my knife and fork at my plate went right into my lap. This confused me still more, and, after drinking one cup of tea, I left the table, and got off to bed as soon as possible. But not a wink of sleep that night. All was confusion, dreams, anxiety, and trembling.

As soon as day dawned, I called for my horse, paid my reckoning, and was on my way, rejoicing that that night was gone, anyhow. I made all diligence on my way, and was across the Ohio, and in Aberdeen by noon, that day!

What my feelings were, when I reached the free shore, can be better imagined than described. I trembled all over with deep emotion, and I could feel my hair rise up on my head. I was on what was called a free soil, among a people who had no slaves. I saw white men at work, and no slave smarting beneath the lash. Everything was indeed new and wonderful. Not knowing where to find a friend, and being ignorant of the country--unwilling to inquire, lest I should betray my ignorance, it was a whole week before I reached Cincinnati. At one place, here I put up, I had a great many more questions put to me than I wished to answer. At another place, I was very much annoyed by the officiousness of the landlord, who made it a point to supply every guest with newspapers. I took the copy handed me, and turned it over, in a somewhat awkward manner, I suppose. He came to me to point out a veto, or some other very important news. I thought it best to decline his assistance, and gave up the paper, saying my eyes were not in a fit condition to read much.

At another place, the neighbors, on learning that a Kentuckian was at the tavern, came, in great earnestness, to find out what my business was. Kentuckians sometimes came there to kidnap their citizens. They were in the habit of watching them close. I at length satisfied them, by assuring them that I was not, nor my father before me, any slaveholder at all; but, lest their suspicious should be excited in another direction, I added, my grandfather was a slaveholder.

At Cincinnati, I found some old acquaintances, and spent several days. In passing through some of the streets, I several times saw a great slave-dealer from Kentucky, who knew me, and, when I approached him, I was very careful to give him a wide berth. The only advice that I here received was from a man who had once been a slave. He urged me to sell my pony, go up the river, to Portsmouth, then take the canal for Cleveland; and cross over to Canada. I acted upon this suggestion, sold my horse for a small sum, as he was pretty well used up, took passage for Portsmouth, and soon found myself on the canal-boat, headed for Cleveland. On the boat, I became acquainted with it Mr. Conoly, from New York. He was very sick with fever and ague, and, as he was a stranger, and alone, I took the best possible care of him, for a time. One day, in conversation with him, he spoke of the slaves, in the most harsh and bitter language, and was especially severe on those who attempted to run away. Thinks I, you are not the man for me to have much to do with. I found the spirit of slaveholding was not all south of the Ohio River.

No sooner had I reached Cleveland, than a trouble came upon me from a very unexpected quarter. A rough, swearing, reckless creature, in the shape of a man, came up to me, and declared I had passed a bad five dollar bill upon his wife, in the boat, and he demanded the silver for it. I had never seen him, nor his wife, before. He pursued me into the tavern, swearing and threatening all the way. The travellers, that had just arrived at the tavern, were asked to give their names to the clerk, that he might enter them upon the book. He called on me for my name, just as this ruffian was in the midst of his assault upon me. On leaving Kentucky, I thought it best, for my own security, to take a new name, and I had been entered on the boat as Archibald Campbell. I knew, with such a charge as this man was making against me, it would not do to change my name from the boat to the hotel. At the moment, I could not recollect what I had called myself, and, for a few minutes, I was in a complete puzzle. The clerk kept calling, and I made believe deaf, till, at length, the name popped back again, and I was duly enrolled a guest at the tavern, in Cleveland. I had heard, before, of persons being frightened out of their Christian names, but I was fairly scared out of both mine for a while. The landlord soon protected me from the violence of the bad-meaning man, and drove him away from the house.

I was detained at Cleveland several days, not knowing how to get across the lake, into Canada. I went out to the shore of the lake again and again, to try and see the other side, but I could see no hill, mountain, nor city of the asylum I sought. I was afraid to inquire where it was, lest it would betray such a degree of ignorance as to excite suspicion at once. One day, I heard a man ask another, employed on board a vessel, "and where does this vessel trade?" Well, I thought, if that is a proper question for you, it is for me. So I passed along, and asked of every vessel, "Where does this vessel trade?" At last, the answer came, "over here in Kettle Creek, near Port Stanley." And where is that? said I. "O, right over here, in Canada." That was the sound for me; "over here in Canada." The captain asked me if I wanted a passage to Canada. I thought it would not do to be too earnest about it, lest it would betray me. I told him I some thought of going, if I could get a passage cheap. We soon came to terms on this point, and that evening we set sail. After proceeding only nine miles, the wind changed, and the captain returned to port again. This, I thought, was a very bad omen. However, I stuck by, and the next evening, at nine o'clock, we set sail once more, and at daylight we were in Canada.

When I stepped ashore here, I said, sure enough, I AM FREE. Good heaven! what a sensation, when it first visits the bosom of a full-grown man; one born to bondage--one who had been taught, from early infancy, that this was his inevitable lot for life. Not till then did I dare to cherish, for a moment, the feeling that one of the limbs of my body was my own. The slaves often say, when cut in the hand or foot, "Plague on the old foot" or "the old hand; it is master's--let him take care of it. Nigger don't care, if he never get well." My hands, my feet, were now my own. But what to do with them, was the next question. A strange sky was over me, a new earth under me, strange voices all around; even the animals were such as I had never seen. A flock of prairie-hens and some black geese were altogether new to me. I was entirely alone; no human being, that I had ever seen before, where I could speak to him or he to me.

And could I make that country ever seem like home? Some people are very much afraid all the slaves will run up north, if they are ever free. But I can assure them that they will run back again, if they do. If I could have been assured of my freedom in Kentucky, then, I would have given any thing in the world for the prospect of spending my life among my old acquaintances, where I first saw the sky, and the sun rise and go down. It was a long time before I could make the sun work right at all. It would rise in the wrong place, and go down wrong; and, finally, it behaved so bad, I thought it could not be the same sun.

There was a little something added to this feeling of strangeness. I could not forget all the horrid stories slaveholders tell about Canada. They assure the slave that, when they get hold of slaves in Canada, they make various uses of them. Sometimes they skin the head, and wear the wool on their coat collars --put them into the lead-mines, with both eyes out--the young slaves they eat; and as for the red coats, they are sure death to the slave. However ridiculous to a well-informed person such stories may appear, they work powerfully upon the excited imagination of an ignorant slave. With these stories all fresh in mind, when I arrived at St. Thomas, I kept a bright look-out for the red coats. As I was turning the corner of one of the streets, sure enough, there stood before me a red coat, in full uniform, with his tall bear-skin cap, a foot and a half high, his gun shouldered, and he standing as erect as a guide-post. Sure enough, that is the fellow that they tell about catching the slave. I turned on my heel, and sought another street. On turning another corner, the same soldier, as I thought, faced me, with his black cap and stern look. Sure enough, my time has come now. I was as near scared to death, then, as a man can be and breathe. I could not have felt any worse if he had shot me right through the heart. I made off again, as soon as I dared to move. I inquired for a tavern. When I came up to it, there was a great brazen lion sleeping over the door, and, although I knew it was not alive, I had been so well frightened that I was almost afraid to go in. Hunger drove me to it at last, and I asked for something to eat.

On my way to St. Thomas I was also badly frightened. A man asked me who I was. I was afraid to tell him a runaway slave, lest he should have me to the mines. I was afraid to say, "I am an American," lest he should shoot me, for I knew there had been trouble between the British and Americans. I inquired, at length, for the place where the greatest number of colored soldiers were. I was told there were a great many at New London; so for New London I started. I got a ride, with some country people, to the latter place. They asked me who I was, and I told them from Kentucky; and they, in a familiar way, called me "Old Kentuck." I saw some soldiers, on the way, and asked the men what they had soldiers for. They said they were kept "to get drunk and be whipped;" that was the chief use they made of them. At last, I reached New London, and here I found soldiers in great numbers. I attended at their parade, and saw the guard driving the people back; but it required no guard to keep me off. I thought, "If you will let me alone, I will not trouble you." I was as much afraid of a red coat as I would have been of a bear. Here I asked again for the colored soldiers. The answer was, "Out at Chatham, about seventy miles distant." I started for Chatham. The first night, I stopped at a place called the Indian Settlement. The door was barred, at the house where I was, which I did not like so well, as I was yet somewhat afraid of their Canadian tricks. Just before I got to Chatham, I met two colored soldiers, with a white man, bound, and driving him along before them. This was something quite new. I thought, then, sure enough, this is the land for me. I had seen a great many colored people bound, and in the hands of the whites, but this was changing things right about. This removed all my suspicions, and, ever after, I felt quite easy in Canada. I made diligent inquiry for several slaves, that I had known in Kentucky, and at length found one, named Henry. He told me of several others, with whom I had been acquainted, and from him, also, I received the first correct information about brother Milton. I knew that he had left Kentucky about a year before I did, and I supposed, until now, that he was in Canada. Henry told me he was at Oberlin, Ohio.

    At Chatham, I hired myself for a while, to recruit my purse a little, as it had become pretty well drained by this time. I had only about sixty-four dollars, when I left Kentucky, and I had been living upon it now for about six weeks. Mr. Everett, with whom I worked, treated me kindly, and urged me to stay in Canada, offering me business on his farm. He declared "there was no 'free state' in America; all were slave states, bound to slavery, and the slave could have no asylum in any of them." There is certainly a great deal of truth in this remark. I have felt, wherever I may be in the United States, the kidnappers may be upon me at any moment. If I should creep up to the top of the monument on Bunker's Hill, beneath which my father fought, I should not be safe, even there. The slave-mongers have a right, by the laws of the United States, to seek me, even upon the top of the monument, whose base rests upon the bones of those who fought for freedom.

I soon after made my way to Sandwich, and crossed over to Detroit, on my way to Ohio, to see Milton. While in Canada, I swapped away my pistol, as I thought I should not need it, for an old watch. When I arrived at Detroit, I found my watch was gone. I put my baggage, with nearly every cent of money I had, on board the boat for Cleveland, and went back to Sandwich to search for the old watch. The ferry here was about three-fourths of a mile, and, in my zeal for the old watch, I wandered so far that I did not get back in season for the boat, and had the satisfaction of hearing her last bell just as I was about to leave the Canada shore. When I got back to Detroit I was in a fine fix; my money and my clothes gone, and I left to wander about in the streets of Detroit. A man may be a man for all clothes or money, but he don't feel quite so well, anyhow. What to do now I could hardly tell. It was about the first of November. I wandered about and picked up something very cheap for supper, and paid nine-pence for lodging. All the next day no boat for Cleveland. Long days and nights to me. At length another boat was up for Cleveland. I went to the Captain, to tell him my story; he was very cross and savage; said a man had no business from home without money; that so many told stories about losing money that he did not know what to believe. He finally asked me how much money I had. I told him sixty-two and a half cents. Well, he said, give me that, and pay the balance when you get there. I gave him every cent I had. We were a day and a night on the passage, and I had nothing to eat except some cold potatoes, which I picked from a barrel of fragments, and cold victuals. I went to the steward, or cook, and asked for something to eat, but he told me his orders were strict to give away nothing, and, if he should do it, he would lose his place at once.

When the boat came to Cleveland it was in the night, and I thought I would spend the balance of the night in the boat. The steward soon came along, asked if I did not know that the boat had landed, and the passengers had gone ashore. I told him I knew it, but I had paid the captain all the money I had, and could get no shelter for the night unless I remained in the boat. He was very harsh and unfeeling, and drove me ashore, although it was very cold, and snow on the ground. I walked around a while, till I saw a light in a small house of entertainment. I called for lodging. In the morning, the Frenchman, who kept it, wanted to know if I would have breakfast. I told him, no. He said then I might pay for my lodging. I told him I would do so before I left, and that my outside coat might hang there till I paid him.

I was obliged at once to start on an expedition for raising some cash. My resources were not very numerous. I took a hairbrush, that I had paid three York shillings for a short time before, and sallied out to make a sale. But the wants of every person I met seemed to be in the same direction with my own; they wanted money more than hairbrushes. At last, I found a customer who paid me nine pence cash, and a small balance in the shape of something to eat for breakfast. I was started square for that day, and delivered out of my present distress. But hunger will return, and all the quicker when a man don't know how to satisfy it when it does come. I went to a plain boarding house, and told the man just my situation; that I was waiting for the boat to return from Buffalo, hoping to get my baggage and money. He said he would board me two or three days and risk it. I tried to get work, but no one seemed inclined to employ me. At last, I gave up in despair, about my luggage, and concluded to start as soon as possible for Oberlin. I sold my great-coat for two dollars, paid one for my board, and with the other I was going to pay my fare to Oberlin. That night, after I had made all my arrangements to leave in the morning, the boat came. On hearing the bell of a steam-boat, in the night, I jumped up and went to the wharf, and found my baggage; paid a quarter of a dollar for the long journey it had been carried, and glad enough to get it again at that.

The next morning, I took the stage for Oberlin; found several abolitionists from that place in the coach. They mentioned a slave named Milton Clarke, who was living there, that he had a brother in Canada, and that he expected him there soon. They spoke in a very friendly manner of Milton, and of the slaves; so, after we had had a long conversation, and I perceived they were all friendly, I made myself known to them. To be thus surrounded at once with friends, in a land of strangers, was something quite new to me. The impression made by the kindness of these strangers upon my heart, will never be effaced. I thought, there must be some new principle at work here, such as I had not seen much of in Kentucky. That evening I arrived at Oberlin, and found Milton boarding at a Mrs. Cole's. Finding here so many friends, my first impression was that all the abolitionists in the country must live right there together. When Milton spoke of going to Massachusetts, "No," said I, "we better stay here where the abolitionists live." And when they assured me that the friends of the slave were more numerous in Massachusetts than in Ohio, I was greatly surprised.

Milton and I had not seen each other for a year; during that time we had passed through the greatest change in outward condition, that can befall a man in this world. How glad we were to greet each other in what we then thought a free State may be easily imagined. We little dreamed of the dangers sleeping around us. Brother Milton had not encountered so much danger in getting away as I had. But his time for suffering was soon to come. For several years before his escape, Milton had hired his time of his master, and had been employed as a steward in different steamboats upon the river. He had paid as high as two hundred dollars a year for his time. From his master he had a written pass, permitting him to go up and down the Mississippi and Ohio rivers when he pleased. He found it easy, therefore, to land on the north side of the Ohio river, and concluded to take his own time for returning. He had caused a letter to be written to Mr. L., his pretended owner, telling him to give himself no anxiety on his account; that he had found by experience he had wit enough to take care of himself, and he thought the care of his master was not worth the two hundred dollars a year which he had been paying for it, for four years; that, on the whole, if his muster would be quiet and contented, he thought he should do very well. This letter, the escape of two persons belonging to the same family, and from the same region, in one year, waked up the fears and the spite of the slaveholders. However, they let us have a little respite, and, through the following winter and spring, we were employed in various kinds of work at Oberlin and in the neighborhood.

All this time I was deliberating upon a plan by which to go down and rescue Cyrus, our youngest brother, from bondage. In July, 1842, I gathered what little money I had saved, which was not a large sum, and started for Kentucky again. As near as I remember, I had about twenty dollars. I did not tell my plan to but one or two at Oberlin, because there were many slaves there, and I did not know but that it might get to Kentucky in some way through them sooner than I should. On my way down through Ohio, I advised with several well-known friends of the slave. Most of them pointed out the dangers I should encounter, and urged me not to go. One young man told me to go, and the God of heaven would prosper me. I knew it was dangerous, but I did not then dream of all that I must suffer in body and mind before I was through with it. It is not a very comfortable feeling, to be creeping round day and night, for nearly two weeks together, in a den of lions, where, if one of them happens to put his paw on you, it is certain death, or something much worse.

At Ripley, I met a man who had lived in Kentucky; he encouraged me to go forward, and directed me about the roads. He told me to keep on a back route not much travelled, and I should not be likely to be molested. I crossed the river at Ripley, and when I reached the other side, and was again upon the soil on which I had suffered so much, I trembled, shuddered, at the thoughts of what might happen to me. My fears, my feelings, overcame for the moment all my resolution, and I was for a time completely overcome with emotion. Tears flowed like a brook of water. I had just left kind friends; I was now where every man I met would be my enemy. It was a long time before I could summon courage sufficient to proceed. I had with me a rude map, made by the Kentuckian whom I saw at Ripley. After examining this as well as I could, I proceeded. In the afternoon of the first day, as I was sitting in a stream to bathe and cool my feet, a man rode up on horseback, and entered into a long conversation with me. He asked me some questions about my travelling, but none but what I could easily answer. He pointed out to me a house where a white woman lived, who, he said, had recently suffered terribly from a fright. Eight slaves, that were running away, called for something to eat, and the poor woman was sorely scared by them. For his part, the man said, he hoped they never would find the slaves again. Slavery was the curse of Kentucky. He had been brought up to work, and he liked to work, but slavery made it disgraceful for any white man to work. From this conversation I was almost a good mind to trust this man, and tell him my story; but, on second thought, I concluded it might be just as safe not to do it. A hundred or two dollars for returning a slave, for a poor man, is a heavy temptation. At night, I stopped at the house of a widow woman, not a tavern, exactly; but they often entertained people there. The next day, when I got as far as Cynthiana, within about twenty miles of Lexington, I was sore all over, and lame, from having walked so far. I tried to hire a horse and carriage, to help me a few miles. At last, I agreed with a man to send me forward to a certain place, which he said was twelve miles, and for which I paid him, in advance, three dollars. It proved to be only seven miles. This was now Sabbath day, as I had selected that as the most suitable day for making my entrance into Lexington. There is much more passing in and out on that day, and I thought I should be much less observed than on any other day.

When I approached the city, and met troops of idlers, on foot and on horseback, sauntering out of the city, I was very careful to keep my umbrella before my face, as people passed, and kept my eyes right before me. There were many persons in the place who had known me, and I did not care to be recognized by any of them. Just before entering the city, I turned off to the field, and lay down under a tree and waited for night.

When its curtains were fairly over me, I started up, took two pocket handkerchiefs, tied one over my forehead, the other under my chin, and marched forward for the city. It was not then so dark as I wished it was. I met a young slave, driving cows. He was quite disposed to condole with me, and said, in a very sympathetic manner, "Massa sick?" "Yes, boy," I said, "Massa sick; drive along your cows." The next colored man I met, I knew him in a moment, but he did not recognize me. I made for the wash-house of the man with whom Cyrus lived. I reached it without attracting any notice, and found there an old slave, as true as steel. I inquired for Cyrus; he said he was at home. He very soon recollected me; and, while the boy was gone to call Cyrus, he uttered a great many exclamations of wonder, to think I should return.

"Good Heaven, boy! what you back here for? What on arth you here for, my son? O, I scared for you! They kill you, just as sure as I alive, if they catch you! Why, in the name of liberty, didn't you stay away, when you gone so slick? Sartin, I never did 'spect to see you again!" I said, "Don't be scared." But he kept repeating, "I scared for you! I scared for you!" When I told him my errand, his wonder was somewhat abated; but still his exclamations were repeated all the evening, "What brought you back here?" In a few minutes, Cyrus made his appearance, filled with little less of wonder than the old man had manifested. I had intended, when I left him, about a year before, that I would return for him, if I was successful in my effort for freedom. He was very glad to see me, and entered, with great animation, upon the plan for his own escape. He had a wife, who was a free woman, and consequently he had a home. He soon went out, and left me in the wash-room with the old man. He went home to apprize his wife, and to prepare a room for my concealment. His wife is a very active, industrious woman, and they were enabled to rent a very comfortable house, and, at this time, had a spare room in the attic, where I could be thoroughly concealed.

He soon returned, and said every thing was ready. I went home with him, and, before ten o'clock at night, I was stowed away in a little room, that was to be my prison-house for about a week. It was a comfortable room; still the confinement was close, and I was unable to take exercise, lest the people in the other part of the house should hear. I got out, and walked around a little, in the evening, but suffered a good deal, for want of more room to live and move in. During the day, Cyrus was busy making arrangements for his departure. He had several little sums of money, in the hands of the foreman of the tan-yard, and in other hands. Now, it would not do to go right boldly up and demand his pay of every one that owed him; this would lead to suspicion at once. So he contrived various ways to get in his little debts. He had seen the foreman, one day, counting out some singular coin of some foreign nation. He pretended to take a great liking to that foreign money, and told the man, if he would pay him what was due him in that money, be would give him two or three dollars. From another person he took an order on a store; and so, in various ways, he got in his little debts as well as he could. At night, we contrived to plan the ways and means of escaping. Cyrus had never been much accustomed to walking, and he dreaded, very much, to undertake such a journey. He proposed to take a couple of horses, as he thought he had richly earned them, over and above all he had received. I objected to this, because, if we were caught, either in Kentucky or out of it, they would bring against us the charge of stealing, and this would be far worse than the charge of running away.

I firmly insisted, therefore, that we must go on foot. In the course of a week, Cyrus had gathered something like twenty dollars, and we were ready for our journey. A family lived in the same house with Cyrus, in a room below. How to get out, in the early part of the evening, and not be discovered, was not an easy question. Finally, we agreed that Cyrus should go down and get into conversation with them, while I slipped out with his bundle of clothes, and repaired to a certain street, where he was to meet me.

As I passed silently out at the door, Cyrus was cracking his best jokes, and raising a general laugh, which completely covered my retreat. Cyrus soon took quiet and unexpected leave of his friends in that family, and leave, also, of his wife above, for a short time only. At a little past eight of the clock we were beyond the bounds of the city. His wife did all she could to assist him in his effort to gain his inalienable rights. She did not dare, however, to let the slaveholders know that she knew anything of his attempt to run away. He had told the slaves that he was going to see his sister, about twelve miles off. It was Saturday night, when we left Lexington. On entering the town, when I went in, I was so intent upon covering up my face, that I took but little notice of the roads. We were very soon exceedingly perplexed to know what road to take. The moon favored us, for it was a clear, beautiful night. On we came, but, at the cross of the roads, what to do we did not know. At length, I climbed one of the guide-posts, and spelled out the names as well as I could. We were on the road to freedom's boundary, and, with a strong step, we measured off the path: but again the cross roads perplexed us. This time, we took hold of the sign-post and lifted it out of the ground, and turned it upon one of its horns, and spelled out the way again. As we started from this goal, I told Cyrus we had not put up the sign-post. He pulled forward, and said he guessed we would do that when we came back. Whether the sign-board is up or down, we have never been there to see.

Soon after leaving the city, we met a great many of the patrols; but they did not arrest us, and we had no disposition to trouble them.

While we were pressing on, by moonlight, and sometimes in great doubt about the road, Cyrus was a good deal discouraged. He thought, if we got upon the wrong road, it would be almost certain death for us, or something worse. In the morning, we found that, on account of our embarrassment in regard to the roads, we had only made a progress of some twenty or twenty-five miles. But we were greatly cheered to find they were so many miles in the right direction. Then we put the best foot forward, and urged our way as fast as possible. In the afternoon it rained very hard; the roads were muddy and slippery. We had slept none the night before, and had been, of course, very much excited. In this state of mind and of body, just before dark, we stopped in a little patch of bushes, to discuss the expediency of going to a house, which we saw at a distance, to spend the night.

As we sat there, Cyrus became very much excited, and, pointing across the road, exclaimed, "Don't you see that animal there?" I looked, but saw nothing; still he affirmed that he saw a dreadful ugly animal looking at us, and ready to make a spring. He began to feel for his pistols, but I told him not to fire there; but he persisted in pointing to the animal, although I am persuaded he saw nothing, only by the force of his imagination. I had some doubts about telling this story, lest people would not believe me; but a friend has suggested to me that such things are not uncommon, when the imagination is strongly excited.

In travelling through the rain and mud, this afternoon, we suffered beyond all power of description. Sometimes we found ourselves just ready to stand, fast asleep, in the middle of the road. Our feet were blistered all over. When Cyrus would get almost discouraged, I urged him on, saying we were walking for freedom now. "Yes," he would say, "freedom is good, Lewis, but this is a hard, h-a-r-d way to get it." This he would say, half asleep. We were so weak, before night, that we several times fell upon our knees in the road. We had crackers with us, but we had no appetite to eat. Fears were behind us; hope before; and we were driven and drawn as hard as ever men were. Our limbs and joints were so stiff that, if we took a step to the right hand or left, it seemed as though it would shake us to pieces. It was a dark, weary day to us both.

At length, I succeeded in getting the consent of Cyrus to go to a house for the night. We found a plain farmer's family. The good man was all taken up in talking about the camp meeting held that day, about three miles from his house. He only asked us where we were from, and we told him our home was in Ohio. He said the young men had behaved unaccountably bad at the camp meeting, and they had but little comfort of it. They mocked the preachers, and disturbed the meeting badly.

We escaped suspicion more readily, as I have no doubt, from the supposition, on the part of many, that we were going to the camp meeting. Next morning, we called at the meeting, as it was on our way, bought up a little extra gingerbread against the time of need, and marched forward for the Ohio. When any one inquired why we left the meeting so soon, we had an answer ready: "The young men behave so bad, we can get no good of the meeting."

By this time we limped badly, and we were sore all over. A young lady whom we met, noticing that we walked lame, cried out, mocking us, "O my feet, my feet, how sore!" At about eleven o'clock, we reached the river, two miles below Ripley. The boatman was on the other side. We called for him. He asked us a few questions. This was a last point with us. We tried our best to appear unconcerned. I asked questions about the boats, as though I had been there before; went to Cyrus, and said, "Sir, I have no change; will you lend me enough to pay my toll? I will pay you before we part." When we were fairly landed upon the northern bank, and had gone a few steps, Cyrus stopped suddenly, on seeing the water gush out at the side of the hill. Said he, "Lewis, give me that tin cup." "What in the world do you want of a tin cup now? We have not time to stop." The cup he would have. Then he went up to the spring, dipped and drank, and dipped and drank; then he would look round, and drink again. "What in the world," said I, "are you fooling there for?" "O," said he, "this is the first time I ever had a chance to drink water that ran out of the free dirt." Then we went a little further, and he sat down on a log. I urged him forward. "O," said he, "I must sit on this free timber a little while."

A short distance further on, we saw a man, who seemed to watch us very closely. I asked him which was the best way to go, over the hill before us, or around it. I did this, to appear to know something about the location. He went off, without offering any obstacles to our journey. In going up the hill, Cyrus would stop, and lay down and roll over. "What in the world are you about, Cyrus? Don't you see Kentucky is over there?" He still continued to roll and kiss the ground; said it was a game horse that could roll clear over. Then he would put face to the ground, and roll over and over. "First time," he said, "he ever rolled on free grass."

After he had recovered a little from his sportive mood, we went up to the house of a good friend of the slave at Ripley. We were weary and worn enough; though ever since we left the river, it seemed as though Cyrus was young and spry as a colt; but when we got where we could rest, we found ourselves tired. The good lady showed us into a good bedroom. Cyrus was skittish. He would not go in and lie down. "I am afraid," said he, "of old mistress. She is too good--too good--can't be so--they want to catch us both." So, to pacify him, I had to go out into the orchard and rest there. When the young men came home, he soon got acquainted, and felt sure they were his friends. From this place we were sent on by the friends, from place to place, till we reached Oberlin, Ohio, in about five weeks after I left there to go for Cyrus. I had encountered a good deal of peril; had suffered much from anxiety of feeling; but felt richly repaid in seeing another brother free.

We stopped at Oberlin a few days, and then Cyrus started for Canada. He did not feel exactly safe. When he reached the lake, he met a man from Lexington who knew him perfectly; indeed, the very man of whom his wife hired her house. This man asked him if he was free. He told him yes, he was free, and he was hunting for brother Milton, to get him to go back and settle with the old man for his freedom. Putnam told him that was all right. He asked Cyrus if he should still want that house his wife lived in. "O, yes," said Cyrus, "we will notify you when we don't want it any more. You tell them, I shall be down there in a few days. I have heard of Milton, and expect to have him soon to carry back with me." Putnam went home, and, when he found what a fool Cyrus had made of him, he was vexed enough, "A rascal," he said, "I could have caught him as well as not."

Cyrus hastened over to Canada. He did not like that country so well as the states, and in a few weeks returned. He had already sent a letter to his wife, giving her an account of his successful escape, and urging her to join him as soon as possible. He had the pleasure of meeting his wife, and her three children by a former husband, and they have found a quiet resting-place, where, if the rumor of oppression reaches them, they do not feel its scourge, nor its chains. And there is no doubt entertained by any of his friends but he can take care of himself.

He begins already to appreciate his rights, and to maintain them as a freeman. The following paragraph concerning him was published in the Liberty Press about one year since:--

"PROGRESS OF FREEDOM

"Scene at Hamilton Village, N. Y.

"Mr. Cyrus Clarke, a brother of the well-known Milton and Lewis Clarke, (all of whom, till within a short time since, for some twenty-five years, were slaves in Kentucky,) mildly, but firmly, presented his ballot at the town meeting board. Be it known that said Cyrus, as well as his brothers, are white, with only a sprinkling of the African; just enough to make them bright, quick, and intelligent, and scarcely observable in the color except by the keen and scenting slaveholder. Mr. Clarke had all the necessary qualifications of white men to vote.

"Slave. Gentlemen, here is my ballot; I wish to vote. (Board and by-standers well knowing him, all were aghast --the waters were troubled--the slave legions were 'up in their might.')

"Judge E. You can't vote! Are you not, and have you not been a slave?

"Slave. I shall not lie to vote. I am and have been a slave, so called; but I wish to vote, and I believe it my right and duty.

"Judge E. Slaves can't vote.

"Slave. Will you just show me in your books, constitution, or whatever you call them, where it says a slave can't vote?

"Judge E. (Pretending to look over the law, &c., well knowing he was 'used up.') Well, well, you are a colored man, and can't vote without you are worth $250.

"Slave. I am as white as you; and don't you vote?

"(Mr. E. is well known to be very dark; indeed, as dark or darker than Clarke. The current began to set against Mr. E. by murmurs, sneers, laughs, and many other demonstrations of dislike.)

"Judge E. Are you not a colored man? and is not your hair curly?

"Slave. We are both colored men; and all we differ is, that you have not the handsome wavy curl; you raise Goat's wool, and I come, as you see, a little nearer Saxony.

"At this time the fire and fun was at its height, and was fast consuming the judge with public opprobrium.

"Judge E. I challenge this man's vote, he being a colored man, and not worth $250.

"Friends and foes warmly contested what constituted a colored man by the New York statute. The board finally came to the honorable conclusion that, to be a colored man, he must be at least one half blood African. Mr. Clarke, the SLAVE, then voted, he being nearly full white. I have the history of this transaction from Mr. Clarke, in person. In substance it is as told me, but varying more or less from his language used.

J. THOMPSON. "PARIS, March, 12, 1844."

Martha, the wife of Cyrus, had a long story of the wrath of the slaveholders, because he ran away. Monday morning she went down, in great distress, to the overseer to inquire for her husband. She, of course, was in great anxiety about him. Mr. Logan threatened her severely, but she, having a little mixture of the Indian, Saxon, and African blood, was quite too keen for them. She succeeded in so far lulling their suspicions as to make her escape, and was very fortunate in her journey to her husband.

We remained but a short time after this in Ohio. I spent a few days in New York; found there a great many warm friends; and, in the autumn of 1843, I came to old Massachusetts. Since that time, I have been engaged a large part of the time in telling the story of what I have felt and seen of slavery.

I have generally found large audiences, and a great desire to hear about slavery. I have been in all the New England States except Connecticut; have held, I suppose, more than five hundred meetings in different places, sometimes two or three in a place. These meetings have been kindly noticed by many of the papers, of all parties and sects. Others have been very bitter and unjust in their remarks, and tried to throw every possible obstacle in my way. A large majority of ministers have been willing to give notice of my meetings, and many of them have attended them. I find that most ministers say they are abolitionists, but truth compels me to add, that, in talking with them, I find many are more zealous to apologize for the slaveholders, than they are to take any active measures to do away slavery.

Since coming to the free states, I have been struck with great surprise at the quiet and peaceable manner in which families live. I had no conception that women could live without quarrelling, till I came into the free states.

After I had been in Ohio a short time, and had not seen nor heard any scolding or quarrelling in the families where I was, I did not know how to account for it. I told Milton, one day, "What a faculty these women have of keeping all their bad feelings to themselves! I have not seen them quarrel with their husbands, nor with the girls, or children, since I have been here." "O," said Milton, "these women are not like our women in Kentucky; they don't fight at all." I told him I doubted that; "I guess they do it somewhere; in the kitchen, or down cellar. It can't be," said I, "that a woman can live, and not scold or quarrel." Milton laughed, and told me to watch them, and see if I could catch them at it. I have kept my eyes and ears open from that day to this, and I have not found the place where the women get mad and rave like they do in Kentucky yet. If they do it here, they are uncommon sly; but I have about concluded that they are altogether different here from what they are in the slave states. I reckon slavery must work upon their minds and dispositions, and make them ugly.

It has been a matter of great wonder to me, also, to see all the children, rich and poor, going to school. Every few miles I see a school-house, here; I did not know what it meant when I saw these houses, when I first came to Ohio. In Kentucky, if you should feed your horse only when you come to a schoolhouse, he would starve to death.

I never had heard a church bell only at Lexington, in my life. When I saw steeples and meeting-houses so thick, it seemed like I had got into another world. Nothing seems more wonderful to me now, than the different way they keep the Sabbath there, and here. In the country, in summer, there the people gather in groups around the meeting-house, built of logs, or around in the groves where they often meet; one company, and perhaps the minister with them, are talking about the price of niggers, pork, and corn; another group are playing cards; others are swapping horses, or horse-racing; all in sight of the meeting-house or place of worship. After a while the minister tells them it is time to begin. They stop playing and talking for a while. If they call him right smart, they hear him out; if he is "no account," they turn to their cards and horses, and finish their devotion in this manner.

The slaveholders are continually telling how poor the white people are in the free states, and how much they suffer from poverty; no masters to look out for them. When, therefore, I came into Ohio, and found nearly every family living in more real comfort than almost any slaveholder, you may easily see I did not know what to make of it. I see how it is now; every man in the free states works; and as they work for themselves, they do twice as much as they would do for another.

In fact, my wonder at the contrast between the slave and the free states has not ceased yet. The more I see here, the more I know slavery curses the master as well as the slave. It curses the soil, the houses, the churches, the schools, the burying-grounds, the flocks, and the herds; it curses man and beast, male and female, old and young. It curses the child in the cradle, and heaps curses upon the old man as he lies in his grave. Let all the people, then, of the civilized world get up upon Mount Ebal, and curse it with a long and bitter curse, and with a loud voice, till it withers and dies; till the year of jubilee dawns upon the south, till the sun of a FREE DAY sends a beam of light and joy into every cabin.

I wish here sincerely to recognize the hand of a kind Providence in leading me from that terrible house of bondage, for raising me up friends in a land of strangers, and for leading me, as I hope, to a saving knowledge of the truth as it is in Christ. A slave cannot be sure that he will always enjoy his religion in peace. Some of them are beaten for acts of devotion. I can never express to God all the gratitude which I owe him for the many favors I now enjoy. I try to live in love with all men. Nothing would delight me more than to take the worst slaveholder by the hand, even Mrs. Banton, and freely forgive her, if I thought she had repented of her sins. While she, or any other man or woman, is trampling down the image of God, and abusing the life out of the poor slave, I cannot believe they are Christians, or that they ought to be allowed the Christian name for one moment. I testify against them now, as having none of the spirit of Christ. There will be a cloud of swift witnesses against them at the day of judgment. The testimony of the slave will be heard then. He has no voice at the tribunals of earthly justice, but he will one day be heard; and then such revelations will be made, as will fully justify the opinion which I have been compelled to form of slaveholders. They are a SEED of evil-doers--corrupt are they--they have done abominable works.

NARRATIVE OF MILTON CLARKE.

PREFACE.

THE Narrative of LEWIS CLARKE was published a year since; and a large edition--three thousand copies--was exhausted in less than a year. There is a call for more; and MILTON CLARKE has concluded to add a few of the incidents of his life, and a more particular account of the attempt to kidnap him in Ohio. I have no doubt, that, with the slight mistakes in regard to circumstances incident to things so long kept only in memory, the following Narrative, as well as that which precedes, may be relied on as true. It is not among the least interesting of the marks of progress in the cause of Freedom, that now, from Ohio, the assistant kidnappers of Jerry Phinney are calling loudly upon their principals in Kentucky to help them out of prison, where they suffer justly. This shows that neither Ohio, nor any other free state, can much longer be made the hunting ground of the slaveholders.

   J. C. L.   May, 1846.

NARRATIVE OF MILTON CLARKE.

WHEN I was about six years of age, the estate of Samuel Campbell, my grandfather, was sold at auction. His sons and daughters were all present at the sale, except Mrs. Banton. Among the articles and animals put upon the catalogue, and placed in the hands of the auctioneer, were a large number of slaves. When every thing else had been disposed of, the question arose among the heirs, "What shall be done with Letty (my mother) and her children?" John and William Campbell came to mother, and told her they would divide her family among the heirs, but none of them should go out of the family. One of the daughters--to her everlasting honor be it spoken-- remonstrated against any such proceeding. Judith, the wife of Joseph Logan, told her brothers and sisters, "Letty is our own half sister, and you know it; father never intended they should be sold." Her protest was disregarded, and the auctioneer was ordered to proceed. My mother, and her infant son Cyrus, about one year old, were put up together and sold for

$500!! Sisters and brothers selling their own sister and her children!! My venerable old father, who was now in extreme old age, and debilitated from the wounds received in the war of the Revolution, was, nevertheless, roused by this outrage upon his rights and upon those of his children.

"He had never expected," he said, "when fighting for the liberties of this country, to see his own wife and children sold in it to the highest bidder." But what were the entreaties of a quivering old man, in the sight of eight or ten hungry heirs? The bidding went on; and the whole family, consisting of mother and eight children, were sold at prices varying from $300 to $800. Lewis, the reader will recollect, had been previously given to that paragon of excellence, Mrs. Banton. It was my fortune, with my mother, brother Cyrus, and sister Delia, to fall into the hands of aunt Judith; and had she lived many years, or had her husband shared with her the virtues of humanity, I should probably have had far less to complain of, for myself and some of the family. She was the only one of all the family that I was ever willing to own, or call my aunt.

The third day after the sale, father, mother, Delia, Cyrus, and myself, started for our home at Lexington, with Mr. Joseph Logan, a tanner. He was a tall, lank, gray-eyed, hard-hearted, cruel wretch; coarse, vulgar, debauched, corrupt and corrupting; but in good and regular standing in the Episcopalian church. We were always protected, however, from any very great hardships during the life of his first wife.

At her death, which happened in about two years, we were sincere mourners; although her husband was probably indulging far other emotions than those of sorrow. He had already entered, to a considerable extent, into arrangements for marrying a younger sister of his wife, Miss Minerva Campbell. She was a half fool, besides being underwitted. If any body falls into such hands, they will know what Solomon meant, when he said, "Let a bear robbed of her whelps meet a man, rather than a fool in his folly." There are a great many bears in Kentucky, but none of them quite equal to a slaveholding woman.

I had a regular battle with this young mistress, when I was about eleven years old. She had lived in the family while her sister was alive, and from the clemency of Judith, in protecting the slaves, the authority of Miss Minerva was in a very doubtful state when she came to be installed mistress of the house. Of course, every occasion was sought to show her authority. She attempted to give me a regular breaking-in, at the age above stated. I used the weapons of defence "God and nature gave me;" I bit and scratched, and well nigh won the battle; but she sent for Logan, whose shadow was more than six feet, and I had to join the non-resistance society right off. It was all day with me then. He dashed me down upon my head, took the raw hide and ploughed up my young back, and that grinning fool, his wife, was looking on; this was a great aggravation of the flogging, that she should see it and rejoice over it.

When I was about twelve years old, I was put to grinding bark in the tannery. Not understanding the business, I did not make such progress as Logan thought I ought to make. Many a severe beating was the consequence. At one time, the shoulder of the horse was very sore, and Logan complained that I did not take good care of him. I tried to defend myself as well as I could, but his final argument was thumping my head against the post. Kings have their last argument, and so have slaveholders. I took the old horse into the stable, and, as I had no one else to talk with, I held quite a dialogue with old Dobbin. Unluckily for me, Logan was hid in another stall, to hear his servant curse him. I told the horse, "Master complains that I don't grind bark enough; complains that I work you too hard; don't feed you enough; now, you old rascal, you know it is a lie, the whole of it; I have given you fifteen ears of corn three times a day, and that is enough for any horse; Cæsar says that is enough, and Moses says that is enough; now eat your corn, and grow fat." At the end of this apostrophe, I gave the old horse three good cuts on the face, and told him to walk up and eat the corn. I then stepped out into the floor and threw in fifteen ears more, and said, "See if the old man will think that is enough."

Scarcely had the words passed my lips, when I heard a rustling in the next stall, and Joe Logan was before me, taller than ever I saw him before, and savage as a cannibal. I made for the door, but he shut it upon me, and caught me by one leg. He began kicking and cuffing, till, in my despair, I seized him, like a young bear, by the leg, with my teeth, and, with all his tearing and wrenching, he could not get me off. He called one of the white hands from the tan-yard, and just as he came in, Logan had his knife out, and was about to cut my throat. The man spoke, and told him not to do that. They tied me and gave me three hundred lashes; my back was peeled from my shoulders to my heels.

Mother was in the house, and heard my screams, but did not dare to come near me. Logan left me weltering in my blood; mother then came and took me up, and carried me into her own room. About 8 o'clock that evening, Logan came out and asked mother if I was alive or dead. She told him I was alive. I laid there four weeks, before I went out of the door. Let fathers and mothers think what it would be to see a child whipped to the very gate of death, and not be permitted to say a word in their behalf. Words can never tell what I suffered, nor what mother suffered. I shuddered at the countenance of Joseph Logan for many months after. The recollection now makes me shudder, as I go back to that bitter day.

Such a cruel wretch could not, of course, manage with much discretion a silly, but high-tempered wife. Their social intercourse was like the meeting of the sirocco and the earthquake. She would scorch terribly with her provoking tongue; he would shake her terribly in his anger. Finally, he held her out at arms length and gave her the horsewhip to the tune of about thirty stripes. She hopped and danced at this, to the infinite amusement of the slaves when we were alone; of course, in their presence we were very serious. We had good reason for rejoicing in this flogging, for she was never known to prescribe raw hide for a slave after that. She soon, however, left her husband and went to live with Mrs. Anderson, where, by her cruelty, she showed her reform was only temporary.

Then began that series of bitter cruelties by which Logan attempted to subdue sister Delia to his diabolical wishes. She was, at this time, some sixteen or eighteen years of age. At first, persuasion was employed. This was soon exchanged for stripes.

One morning, I was a witness of the torture which he inflicted. Sister asked me to speak to mother; I ran and called her; she hesitated a good deal, but the shrieks of her child at length overcame every fear, and she rushed into the presence of, and began to remonstrate with, this brute. He was only the more enraged. He turned around with all the vengeance of a fury, and knocked poor mother down, and injured her severely; when I saw the blood streaming from the shoulders of my sister, and my mother knocked down, I became completely frantic, and ran and caught an axe, and intended to cut him down at a blow. My mother had recovered her feet just in time to meet me at the door. She persuaded me not to go into the spinning-room, where this whipping took place. Sister soon came out, covered with blood. Mother washed her wounds as well as she could. In six days after this, sister was chained to a gang of a hundred and sixty slaves, and sent down to New Orleans. Mother begged for her daughter; said she would get someone to buy her; a gentleman offered to do this, after she was sold to the slave-driver; but the inhuman monster was inexorable; this was the punishment threatened, if he was refused the sacrifice of her innocence.

Sister was therefore carried down the river to New Orleans, kept three or four weeks, and then put up for sale. The day before the sale, she was taken to the barber's, her hair dressed, and she was furnished with a new silk gown, and gold watch, and every thing done to set off her personal attractions, previous to the time of the bidding. The first bid was $500; then $800. The auctioneer began to extol her virtues. Then $1000 was bid. The auctioneer says, "If you only knew the reason why she is sold, you would give any sum for her. She is a pious, good girl, member of the Baptist church, warranted to be a virtuous girl." The bidding grew brisk. "Twelve!" "thirteen," "fourteen," "fifteen," "sixteen hundred," was at length bid, and she was knocked off to a Frenchman, named Coval. He wanted her to live with him as his housekeeper and mistress. This she utterly refused, unless she were emancipated and made his wife. In about one month, he took her to Mexico, emancipated, and married her. She visited France with her husband, spent a year or more there and in the West Indies. In four or five years after her marriage, her husband died, leaving her a fortune of twenty or thirty thousand dollars. A more just and remarkable reward of sterling virtue in an unprotected girl, cannot be found in all the books of romance.

But I must return to my own story. Soon after the sale of my sister, the father of Joseph Logan, Deacon Archibald Logan, purchased his estate in Lexington, and all his slaves; mother, Cyrus, and myself, among the number. I was then valued at one thousand dollars. Mother, I should rather say, was given away in her old age to old Mrs. Logan, the wife of the deacon. In three or four years after this, Joseph Logan came to the house of his father, sick with the consumption, and died. He professed to be penitent upon his death-bed, and asked forgiveness of mother and myself for all the wrong done to our family.

I was then taken by the deacon for his body servant; travelled with him, and was often supposed to be his son.

I have little complaint to make of the old man, except that he kept me a slave. Cyrus was put into the tanyard, and fared very differently. For some reason, the old deacon treated him with great cruelty.

In 1833, my poor mother ended her sorrows, cut off very suddenly by the cholera. Our condition was then desolate indeed. Father had died several years before. The prospect before us was interminable, lonely bondage. The thought of it sometimes drove us almost to despair. I soon began to hire my time, by the day, or week, as I could make a bargain. I was a very good bass drummer, and had learned to play on the bugle. The deacon would hire me out to play for volunteers, that were then and soon after training for a campaign in Texas. He received three dollars for half a day for my services. When I found this out, I sold my bugle and drum. He was very sorry I had sold them; would have bought them himself, if he had known I wanted to sell. I told him, I was tired of playing. We soon compromised the matter, however; I bought my instruments, and was to have half I earned with them. I then began to lay up money, and had a shrewd notion that I could take care of myself. I frequently heard the Declaration of Independence read; and listened with great wonder to the Texas orators, as they talked about liberty. I thought it might be as good for me as for others. I could never reason myself into the belief, that the old deacon had any right to the annual rent which I paid for my own body. I then was paying to this old miser two hundred dollars a year for my time, boarding and clothing myself. I joined a company of musicians, and we made money fast and easy by attending balls and parties.

But before leaving the deacon, I wish to give a few recollections of his family matters, to illustrate the workings of good society among slaveholders. The deacon lost his wife about the time of the death of my mother. He was an older of the Presbyterian church, and afterwards became at deacon of a Congregational church; and there was a widow named Robb, of the same communion; a good name for the whole clan of slaveholding tyrants, male and female; they are all robbers of the worst kind. The good women of the deacon's acquaintance visited him, and pitied his lonely condition, and hinted, that Mrs. Robb would be a great comfort to him in his affliction.

The negotiation was commenced, and soon terminated, to the present satisfaction of both parties. But two old people, with habits firmly fixed, do not often, like kindred drops, mingle into one. Each one wanted to keep their household fixings for their own children.

She was younger than the deacon, more artful, and could easily outwit him. The daughters of Mr. Logan had come to the house, before the marriage, and carefully marked the bedding. The deacon gave me the keys of his rooms, and attempted to limit the freedom of his new spouse in the house of which she was installed mistress. This produced confusion and abundance of sparring. She treated her slaves better than she did his, and this set all the old servants against her. She got to the old man's closet, drank his wine, and then charged it to the slaves. We were not long in pointing out to the deacon the true channel in which his wine flowed. Her servants were frequently dispatched, with buckets of sugar and coffee, to the daughters of Mrs. Logan. It was nuts for us to find this out and tell the deacon. Here was new fuel for the fires of dispute that crackled every day in this habitation of the Patriarchs. They quarreled openly; it was a public scandal; till, one day, his old withered hand seized the horsewhip and crowned their bliss with a dozen or two good smart lashes. The flame was all abroad, then. Many waters could not quench the fires of this loving pair. She left him, and her son-in-law threatened the old man's back with the cow-skin.

The church interposed and called him to account. He owned up, as to the whipping; but justified, under the plea, that he afflicted the body for the good of the soul. It would not do. He bought off from his wife, and she left him. The church excommunicated the deacon. He made application, very soon, for admission to a Congregational church. They would not receive him, till he made some sort of a confession. He acknowledged the fact, but plead a good motive--the benefit of her soul. He was at length received, and presently began to garner the sanctuary of oppression--a southern church. The house was soon carpeted; the pulpit was renovated, dressed in velvet; a new bell bung, and new life infused into the waning church, which had just received such an ornament to its virtues and holiness. The unlucky minister had a little bit of decency, if not of conscience left. He had opposed the whole proceeding. Educated at the north, he one day dropped some word of condemnation of the sin of oppression. This was too much for the deacon. The minister was forthwith dismissed, and a more supple tool employed. The old man could hardly be trained to the exemplary habits becoming an office-bearer of the standards of Zion. Frequent attempts were made to discipline him; but the deacon, with his great wealth, had such ascendency over the minds of his brethren, that a vote of censure or suspension could never be obtained. He lived and died in "good and regular standing," so far as came to my knowledge or belief.

The only beating that I had, after I came into the hands of Deacon Logan, was at the instigation of his son Joseph. Only about thirty lashes were put on by the public whipper, in the watch-house. I was tied, hands and feet, and whipped by the servile wretch, who does this business at a dollar a head for men--the same for women.

I did not witness as many scenes of cruelty among the slaves as many have; I was usually employed about the house, and was not in a situation to see what others have. One or two instances I can mention of what I personally knew of the cruelty of slaveholders. Joseph Logan had a slave, named Priscilla. She did the work in the kitchen. One morning, the biscuit came upon the table badly scorched. Mistress Minerva threw them in her face, struck her with the shovel, then heated the tongs, and took her by the nose. She raised her hand, to resist this act of wanton cruelty. Logan was called for, came out, and knocked her down with a large club; called in his men, and had her tied and beaten most unmercifully. He then put a log chain on her, and compelled her to drag it for days. She never recovered; her mind was destroyed, and she was soon after sold, for little or nothing, as an idiot.

Joseph Logan had another slave, named Peter. The wife of Peter was the slave of Thomas Kennedy, who lived forty-five miles from Lexington. Kennedy consented to sell Milly only on condition that, if she was ever resold, he should have the refusal of her. She lived with her husband till she had two children, and then her mistress, Minerva, resolved she should be sold. The tears and entreaties of her husband, the despair upon the countenance of the victim herself, were all in vain. She, with her two children, was sold to Warren Orford, one of the soul drivers, for twelve or thirteen hundred dollars. The husband became melancholy, sank down under his burden, turned to the intoxicating cup, and became a drunkard.

In the year 1838, I hired my time of Deacon Logan, for the purpose of going in a steamboat up and down the Ohio and Mississippi Rivers. I was at New Orleans three or four times, before I could find anything of sister Delia. At last, through the assistance of an old acquaintance, I found where she lived. I went to the house, but I was so changed, by the growth of seven or eight years, that she did not know me. When I told her who I was, she was very incredulous; and, to test my identity, brought forward a small article of clothing, and asked me if ever I had seen it. I told her it once belonged to mother. "Ah! then," she said, "you must be my brother." She was very glad to see me, and hear from her brothers and sisters.

The next summer, she visited Kentucky with me, and spent two or three months. Deacon Logan treated her with great politeness; said his son did very wrong to sell her as he did; that, if he had then owned the family, it should not have been done. While in Kentucky, she advanced the money, in part, to pay for the freedom of Dennis, and, as soon as she returned to New Orleans, she sent up the balance.

She also made arrangements with Deacon Logan, to purchase brother Cyrus and myself for sixteen hundred dollars.

In the autumn of 1840, I started to go to New Orleans, to get the money to pay for Cyrus and myself. When I arrived at Louisville, I met the sorrowful tidings that sister was dead! This was a sudden, withering blast of all my well-founded hopes of deliverance from slavery. The same letter that brought the tidings of her death also informed me that she had left her property, by will, to me, for the purpose of buying myself, and all the family, from bondage. I was now told that, if I went down and took the property, my master could claim and take the whole of it. I went directly back to Lexington, and asked Mr. Logan to make me free, and I would pay him a thousand dollars, the first money that I received from the estate of my sister. This he said he would not do; but he gave me a free paper, to pass up and down the river as I pleased, and to transact any business as though I was free. With this paper, I started for New Orleans, but could get no more than sixty dollars and a suit of clothes. The person with whom it was left, said it was in real estate, and he had no authority to sell it. I then began to think that the day of my freedom was a great way off. I concluded, with a great many other persons in desperate circumstances, to go to Texas. I took boat for Galveston. Here it looked worse than slavery, if anything can be worse. I soon returned, and came up to Louisville. Here I met three slaves of Doctor Graham, of Harrodsburg, Kentucky. Their names were Henry, Reuben, and George; all smart, fine fellows, good musicians, and yielding the doctor a handsome income. In the same company were three others, all of the same craft.

"Now," said I, "boys, is the time to strike for liberty. I go for Ohio to-morrow. What say you?" They pondered the question, and we all determined to start, as a company of musicians, to attend a great ball in Cincinnati--and, sure enough, it was the grandest ball we ever played for. We came to Cincinnati, and the friends there advised us to go farther north. Doctor Graham's boys struck for Canada, while I stopped at Oberlin, Ohio. It was well they did, for the doctor was close upon them, offering a large reward. He reached Detroit within a few hours after they had crossed the ice to Malden. He attempted to hire some one to go over, and capture them; no one would attempt this. He hired a man, at last, to go over and hire them to get on a boat, and go to Toledo, to play for a ball. Doctor Graham was to be in the boat, when it touched at Malden. For some reason, the boys were quite cautious, and very reluctant to go. When the wolf in sheep's clothing offered them five hundred dollars to go and play for one ball, they were more suspicious than ever. When the boat touched at the wharf, the boys were on the wharf, playing a gypsy waltz, a great favorite of Doctor Graham's. When the doctor found his plan did not work, sure enough, he came out to hear his favorite singers. He landed, and spent several days in fruitless endeavors to persuade them to return to Kentucky. They still persist in preferring a monarchy to the patriarchal form of government.

While at Oberlin, there was an attempt to capture a Mr. Johnson and his wife, residents in that place. They had once, to be sure, had a more southern home; but they believed the world was free for them to choose a home in, as well as for others. Johnson worked in a blacksmith's shop, with another man. To this individual he confided the name and place of the robber who had claimed him in Ohio. This wretch went to another, blacker-hearted one, named Benedict, of Illyria. Let no mother ever use that name again for her new-born son. It was disgraced enough by Benedict Arnold--it should, with him, be covered in oblivion. But this lawyer, Benedict of Illyria, has made the infamy around that name thicker and blacker than it was before. He wrote to the pretended owner of Johnson where he could be found. In hot haste he came; but, thanks to an honest justice, his evidence was not sufficient. He returned for better testimony; as he came back, he was suddenly grasped by the hand of death, and died within ten miles of Oberlin, with an oath upon his lips. Johnson and his wife broke jail, and were carried forward to Canada. There were a great many forwarding houses in Ohio at that time; they have greatly increased since, and nearly all of them are doing a first-rate business.

During the summer of 1841, the emigration to Canada, through Oberlin, was very large. I had the pleasure of giving the "right hand of fellowship" to a goodly number of my former acquaintances and fellow-sufferers. The masters accused me of stealing several of them. This is a great lie. I never stole one in my life. I have assisted several to get into possession of the true owner, but I never assisted any man to steal another away from himself. God has given every man the true title-deed to himself, written upon his face. It cannot be blotted entirely out. The slaveholders try hard to do it, but it can yet be read; all other titles are shams and forgeries. Among others, I assisted a Mrs. Swift, and her two children, to get over to Canada, where they can read titles more clearly than they do in some of the states. This was brought up as a heavy charge against me by Mr. Postlewaite, the illustrious catchpole of the slaveholders.

In the autumn of this year, I was delighted to meet brother Lewis at Oberlin. The happiness which we both experienced at meeting each other, as we supposed, securely free, in a free state, may be well imagined.

In 1842, there were nine slaves reached Oberlin by one arrival, all from one plantation. A Mr. Benningale, of Kentucky, was close upon them, impiously claiming that he had property in these images of God; ay, that they were property, and entirely his, to all intents and purposes. This is not the doctrine taught by a great many good men in Ohio. These men came to Oberlin. The next day, Benningale arrived. He lined the lake with watchmen. **Benedict** (do, printers, put that name in black type, if you can) of Illyria was on the alert; thirty pieces of silver were always the full price of innocent blood with him. Benningale, finding they were hid in the village, threatened to burn the town. The colored people were on guard all night. They met two persons, whom they suspected as spies of the kidnappers. They told them, if they caught them out again, they should be hung right up, as spies against liberty. The fugitives were at length put into a wagon, carried to the lake, and shipped for Canada. The pursuers offered a thousand dollars for their arrest. No one was found sufficiently enterprising to claim the reward. They landed safe upon the other side. Soon after this, there were seven more slaves arrived at Oberlin. The miserable Benedict, assisted by the Chapmans, set their traps around the village. Seven hundred dollars reward was offered for their arrest. Power of attorney had been sent on to the traitor Benedict. The slaves were kept concealed, till, as in the case of Moses, it was no longer safe for them. There were six men and one woman in the company. A plan was contrived to put the kidnappers upon a false scent. Six colored men were selected to personate the men, and I was dressed in female attire, to be passed off for the woman. A telltale was informed that the slaves would start for the lake at such a time, and go in a certain direction. He was solemnly enjoined not to tell a word of it. Those who knew him understood what he would do. The secret was too precious for him to keep. He ran right to Benedict with it. We left Oberlin in one direction, and the real objects of pursuit started, soon after, upon another road. The ruse took; Benedict and Company were in full pursuit, with sheriff, writ, and all the implements of kidnapping. We selected one of our number, George Perry, to act as spokesman for the gang. Just as we arrived at the village of Illyria, eight miles from Oberlin, Benedict and Company surrounded our carriage, and ordered the driver to stop. Platt, the driver, challenged his authority. Benedict pulled out his advertisement, six men and one woman, with the description of their persons. Platt told him he thought they were not the persons he was after. The traitor affirmed he knew they were. The driver turned to his passengers, and said he could do no more for them. George then began to play his part: "Well, 'den, 'dis nigger must get out." We accordingly left the carriage, and were conducted into the tavern. In the tavern were two travellers, who were very inquisitive. "Where are you from?" George answered, "Don't care where I from." Benedict, when he began to suspect that all was not exactly right, came up to me for a more minute examination of my person. I had kept my head and face under my hood and cloak. He ordered me to hold up my head. George says, "Let 'dat gal alone, Mr. white man; de nigger gal plague enough in slave state--you just let her alone, here, if you please." One of the travellers called for cider; George stepped up and drank it for him. The table was furnished for some of the guests, and George, without any ceremony, declared "'Dis nigger hungry," and swept the table for himself and comrades. The landlord threatened to flog him. The colored men all spoke up together, "\You strike 'dat nigger if you dare." At last, they got a justice of the peace; but he had been let into the whole secret. Benedict began his plea; produced his evidence; said that ungrateful girl (pointing to me) had left a kind mistress, right in the midst of a large ironing!!! The justice finally said, he did not see but he must give us up to Mr. Benedict as slaves, fugitives from service. Our friends then gave the signal, and I threw off my bonnet and cloak, and stood up a man. Such a shout as the spectators raised would do the heart of freedom good. "Why, your woman has turned into a man, Mr. Benedict." "It may be these others, that appear to be men, are all women." Benedict saw through the plot, and took his saddle without any rejoinder to his plea. The tavern-keeper ordered us out of the house, and we took carriage for Oberlin. Meanwhile the real objects of pursuit were sailing on the waters of the blue lake.

Benedict was terribly angry at me. He swore he would have me captured. He wrote immediately to Deacon Logan, that no slaves could be captured there while Milton Clarke was at large.

The slaveholders of Lexington had a meeting, and determined to send a Mr. Postlewaite, a crack slave-breaker, and a Mr. M'Gowan, after me. They came and lingered about Oberlin, watching their opportunity. They engaged two wretches named Chapman, of Illyria, to assist in the capture. Brother Lewis and I went up to Madison, Lake county, to spend a few days. We had a meeting on Sabbath evening, at which we addressed the people. There was a traitor there named Warner, from Lexington, who told Postlewaite where we were. Monday morning, my brother and myself rode up to Dr. Merriam's, accompanied by two or three of Mr. Winchester's family, with whom we had spent the Sabbath. I sat a few minutes in the carriage; and a little girl out of health, the niece of Dr. Merriam, and his own daughter, came out and wanted to ride. I took them in, and had not driven a mile when a close carriage overtook and passed me, wheeled right across the road, and four men leaped out of it and seized my horse. I had no conjecture who they were. I asked them what they wanted--"if money, I have only fifty cents in the world; you are welcome to that." "We want not money, but you!" The truth then flashed upon my mind in a moment-- "They are kidnappers."

I jumped from the carriage for the purpose of running for life. My foot slipped, and I fell. In a moment, four men were upon me. They thrust my head down upon the ground, bound me hand and foot, put me into the carriage, and started for Judge Page's; a judge prepared beforehand for their purposes. Soon after we started, we met a man in the road. I spoke to him, and asked him to take care of the girls in the buggy, and to tell Lewis the kidnappers from Kentucky had got me. Postlewaite and M'Gowan took off my hat, and gave me a beating upon the head. One of the Chapmans spoke and said, "Now we have got you, my good fellow; you are the chap that has enticed away so many slaves; we will take care of you; we will have Lewis soon." They then took me to Mr. Judge Page. The sheriff of the county was there. He asked me what I had done, that they had tied me up so close.

"Have you murdered any body?" I said, "No." "Have you been stealing?" "No, sir." "What have you done?" "Nothing, sir." "What have they tied you for, then?" Postlewaite told him it was none of his business. The sheriff said it was his business, and, "if he has committed no crime, you must untie him." He then came up to take off the cords from me. Postlewaite drew his pistols, and threatened to shoot him. Judge Page told the sheriff lie had better not touch the gentleman's property. The sheriff said he would see whose property he was. By this time the alarm was spread, and a large company had gathered around the tavern. The sheriff told the people to see that that man was not removed till he came back. He went out, and summoned the posse of farmers in every direction. They left their ploughs, and jumped upon their horses, with the collars yet on their necks, and rode with all speed for the scene of action. "The kidnappers had got the white nigger," was the watchword.

Postlewaite began to be alarmed. He asked Mr. Page which was the best way for him to go. Could he go safely to the lake, and take a steamboat for Cleveland? "Why, no, the abolitionists watch all the landing-places." Could he go to Painesville? "Why, no, General Paine, a red-hot abolitionist, is there." Postlewaite asked for a place to take me, where I should be secure. They carried me to the counting-room of the judge. They then began to coax. The judge said, "You better go back, Clarke, willingly; it will be better for you, when you get there." "Did not your master treat you well?" asked the very gracious Mr. Postlewaite. "Yes," I said, "he treated me well; no fault to find with him on that score." "What did you run away for, then?" "I came, sir, to get my freedom. I offered him eight hundred dollars for my liberty, and he would not take it. I had paid him about that much for my time, and I thought I might as well have what I earned, as to pay it to him." "Well, sir, if you had come off alone, the deacon would not have cared so much about it; but you led others off; and now we are going to carry you back, and whip you, on the public square in Lexington."

The judge had appointed three o'clock in the afternoon for my trial, as my friends said they wished to procure evidence that I came away with the consent of Deacon Logan. In the meantime, Postlewaite & Co. were full of joy at their success, and despatched a letter to Lexington, announcing the capture of Milton Clarke, and assuring their friends there, that they should have Lewis before sundown. "We shall be in Lexington with them about Thursday or Friday." This was great news to the deacon and his friends; but, alas for them, the result was not exactly to answer to the expectation. They assembled in great numbers on both days, as I have been told, and watched, with eager interest, the arrival of the stage; but no Clarke, and no Postlewaite, were in it. Many a triumph has been enjoyed only in anticipation.

Dinner came on, at length, and I was moved back into the tavern. Postlewaite had a rope around me, which he kept in his hand all the time. They called for dinner for six-- the driver and myself among the number. When they sat down, I was placed at a short distance from the table. The landlady asked if I was not to sit down. Postlewaite said, no nigger should sit at table with him. She belabored him in good womanly style; told him he was a thief, and a scoundrel, and that, if she was a man, he should never carry me away. The people were gathered, all this time, around the windows, and in the road, discussing the matter, and getting up the steam, to meet the Kentucky bowie knives and pistols. Postlewaite sent out, and got a man to come in and watch me, while he eat his dinner, The people at the windows were preparing to take me out. He watched the movement, and had me brought up nearer to the table.

At three o'clock, my trial came on. My friends claimed, that I should have a trial as a white man. Robert Harper plead for the oppressors, assisted by another, whose name is unknown to me. For me, lawyer Chase, and another, appeared. To these gentlemen, and all others, who were friendly to me on this occasion, I feel an obligation which I can never express. It was to me, indeed, a dark hour, and they were friends in time of need. General Paine arrived about the commencement of the trial, and presented a firm front to the tyrants. My lawyer asked by what law they claimed me. They said, under the black law of Ohio. The reply was, that I was not a black man. Postlewaite said he arrested me, as the property of Archibald Logan, under the article of the constitution, that persons "owing service," and fleeing from one state to another, shall be given up to the person to whom such service is due. He then read the power of attorney, from Deacon Logan to him, authorizing him to seize one Milton Clarke--describing me as a person five feet two and a half inches tall, probably trying to pass myself off as white. "His hair is straight, but curls a little at the lower end." After reading this, he read his other papers, showing that I was the slave of Logan. He produced a bill of sale, from Joseph to Deacon Logan. He then asked me if I had not lived, for several years, with Deacon Logan. General Paine said, if I spoke at all, I might tell the whole story-- that I had a free pass to go where I chose, (and this was the fact.) The suggestion of General Paine frightened Postlewaite; he told me to shut up my jaws, or he would smash my face in for me. The people cried out, "Touch him if you dare; we will string you up, short metre." He then said to me, "D--n you; we will pay you for all this, when we get home." The anxiety on my part, by this time, was beyond anything I ever felt in my life. I sometimes hoped the people would rescue me, and then feared they would not. Many of them showed sympathy in their countenances, and I could see that the savageism of Postlewaite greatly increased it. My lawyer then asked, for what I owed service to Deacon Logan; told Harper & Co., if Mr. Clarke owed the deacon, present his bill, and, if it is a reasonable one, his friends will pay it. He then asked me if I owed Deacon Logan, of Kentucky. I told him no--the deacon owed me about eight hundred dollars; I owed him nothing. Postlewaite said, then, he arrested me as the goods and chattels of Logan. Mr. Chase said, "Mr. Clarke had permission to come into the free states." "Yes," said Postlewaite, "but not to stay so long." Finally, Mr. Chase asked, "Where did Joseph Logan get his right to Clarke?" On this point, he had no specific evidence. He then resorted to the general testimony of several letters, which he took from his pocket. One was from General Coombs, another from McCauly, one from John Crittenden, one from Morehead, Governor Lecher, John Speed Smith, and, last of all, from HENRY CLAY. These gentlemen all represented Mr. Postlewaite as a most pious and excellent man, whose word was to be taken in every thing; stating, also, that they knew Milton Clarke, and that he was the property of Deacon A. Logan. This array of names closed the testimony. Bob Harper then made his infamous plea; said, finally, the judge could possibly do no otherwise than give me up, on the testimony of so many great names. Judge Page had received his fee, as I verily believe, before he gave judgment; and he very soon came to the conclusion, that

Deacon Logan had proved his claim. I was delivered over to the tender mercies of Postlewaite & Co. Just as we were going out at the door, the sheriff met us, and arrested Postlewaite, McGowan, and the Chapmans, for assault and battery on the person of Milton Clarke. They were told, their trial would come on the next day, at ten o'clock, before Justice Cunningham. Postlewaite swore terribly at this; said it was an abolition concern. Someone asked the sheriff what should be done with me. He said he did not want me --it was the others that he had arrested. I was then tied to Postlewaite. Someone said, "Cut him loose." Postlewaite replied, "The first that attempts to touch him, I will blow him through." I asked the people if I should be carried back, as I had committed no crime. They said, "No, no; never." General Paine said he would call out the militia, before I should be carried back.

Postlewaite ordered out his carriage, to accompany the sheriff. He drove me into it, came in with his partners, McGowan and the Chapmans, and Judge Page. We then started for Unionville, distant about two miles from Centreville. A very great crowd followed us, on every side. My friends had not been idle; they had been over to Jeffersonville, in Ashtabula county, and obtained a writ of Habeas Corpus for me. Unionville was upon the border of two counties. The road through it divided them. The people had fixed their carriages so that ours must pass upon the Ashtabula side. Soon as the wheels passed the border of this county, the carriage was stopped, and the sheriff of Ashtabula demanded the body of Milton Clarke. The people shouted, came up and unhitched the horses, and turned them face to the carriage. Postlewaite cried out, "Drive on." Driver replied, "The horses are faced about." P. began to be very angry. The people asked the driver what he was there for, assisting in such business as this. The poor fellow begged they would not harm his horses; he did not know what they wanted him for, or he never would have come. He begged for his horses, and himself. Postlewaite said, if they meddled with the horses, he would shoot a hundred of them. The people told him, if he put his head out of that carriage, he would never shoot again. At this stage of the business, Robert Harper, Esq., came up, to read the riot act. The people were acting under a charter broader and older than any statutes passed on earth. Harper was glad to escape himself, or justice would have speedily been meted out to him. The friends came up to the carriage, and told me not to be alarmed; they would have me, at any rate. Among others in the crowd, was a huge Buckeye blacksmith, six feet tall. At first, he took sides with the thieves; said he wanted no niggers there. My friends told him to come up to the carriage, and pick out the nigger, if there was any there. He came, and looked into the carriage some time, and at last, pointing to Postlewaite, said, "That is the nigger." The chivalric Mr. P. told him no man called him nigger with impunity. The Buckeye insisted upon it he was the nigger. P. told him he lied, three times. The northern lion was waked up, and he slapped the armed knight in the face. Postlewaite drew his bowie knife, and threatened to cut him. The Ohioan asked him what it was. He said, a bowie knife. "What are you going to do with it?" "Put it into you, if you put your head in here again." "Ay, ay, you are going to booy me, are you? Then I'll booy you." He ran to the fence, and seized a sharp rail, and said he was going to booy, too. The sheriff, that had the writ to take me, let down the steps; and the people called out, "Let us kill them." The man armed with the rail, began to beat the door, and told them to let me out. General Paine spoke, and urged the multitude not to proceed to violence. Judge Page began to feel quite uneasy, in his new position. He exhorted me to keep still, or they would kill us all. The sheriff then gave Postlewaite and Company five minutes' time to release me, or take the consequences; said the carriage would be demolished in two minutes, when he spoke the word to the people. The pistols and bowie knives were quietly put away, and the tone of the stationary passengers, inside the carriage, very suddenly changed. Judge Page said, "Better let Clarke get out; they will kill us, if you don't." The cowardly Chapmans began to plead for mercy: "You can't say that we touched you, Clarke." "Yes you did," I told them; "you all jumped on me at once." The people became more and more clamorous outside the carriage--those inside more and more uneasy. They at length were more eager to get rid of me than they ever had been to catch me. "Get out; get out, Clarke," rung round on every side of me.

Soon as my feet touched the ground, the rope was cut, and once more I felt free. I was hurried into a wagon, and, under the care of the sheriff, driven off toward Austinburg, while the other sheriff took the kidnappers in another direction into Lake county. They soon stopped to give me something to eat; but I had no appetite for food, either then or for a week afterwards.

Postlewaite hired a man to follow and watch me. But my friends soon contrived to put him on a false scent. It was now dark, and I exchanged seats with a Mr. Winchester, and the watch-dog soon found he was on the wrong trail. The sheriff that had me in keeping was not very careful of his charge, and he soon lost all knowledge of my whereabouts. I was concealed for two or three days at Austinburg, as lonely as mortal man could well be. One night I went out and slept upon the haystack in the field, fearing they might search the house. The man who owned it came next day to Mr. Austin's, where I stopped, to know if it was so; said, if he had known that a nigger slept there, he would have burned the hay and him all up together. "Let him go back, where he belongs."

He then turned to me, and asked me if I had seen that nigger. I told him I had; I knew him very well. Mr. Austin asked him what he would say, if they should come and attempt to take me into slavery; why, said he, "I would shoot them." His philanthropy was graduated, like many others, upon nothing more substantial than color.

In a few days I had the pleasure to learn that Postlewaite and Company, after a trial before Mr. Cunningham, had returned to Kentucky. I have since been told they crept into the city of Lexington as silently as possible; that they left the stage before it entered the city, and went in under the shade of night. When they were visible, the inquiries were thick and fast, "Where are the Clarkes? What have you done with the Clarkes?"

Both the little girls in the carriage when I left it were thrown out, and one so injured that she never recovered. She died in a few days.

The citizens called a meeting at Austinburg, and Lewis and I began to lecture on the subject of slavery. From that time to the present, we have had more calls for meetings than we could attend. We have been in eight different states, and hundreds of thousands have listened with interest to the story of our wrongs, and the wrongs of our countrymen in bonds. If God spares our lives, we hope to see the day when the trump of jubilee shall sound, and liberty shall be proclaimed throughout the land to all the inhabitants thereof.

APPENDIX.

A SKETCH OF THE CLARKE FAMILY.

BY LEWIS CLARKE.

MY mother was called a very handsome woman. She was very much esteemed by all who knew her; the slaves looked up to her for advice. She died, much lamented, of the cholera, in the year 1833. I was not at home, and had not even the melancholy pleasure of following her to her grave.

1. The name of the oldest member of the family was Archy. He never enjoyed very good health, but was a man of great ingenuity, and very much beloved by all his associates, colored and white. Through his own exertions, and the kindness of C. M. Clay, and one or two other friends, he procured his freedom. He lived to repay Mr. Clay and others the money advanced for him, but not long enough to enjoy for many years the freedom for which he had struggled

so hard. He paid six hundred dollars for himself. He died about seven years since, leaving a wife and four or five children in bondage; the inheritance of the widow and poor orphans is, LABOR WITHOUT WAGES; WRONGS WITH NO REDRESS; SEPARATION FROM EACH OTHER FOR LIFE, and no being to hear their complaint, but that God who is the widow's God and Judge. "Shall I not be avenged on such a nation as this?"

2. Sister Christiana was next to Archy in age. She was first married to a free colored man. By him she had several children. Her master did not like this connection, and her husband was driven away, and told never to be seen there again. The name of her master is Oliver Anderson; he is a leading man in the Presbyterian church, and is considered one of the best among slaveholders. Mr. Anderson married Polly Campbell, at the time I was given to Mrs. Betsey Banton. I believe she and Mrs. Banton have not spoken together since they divided the slaves at the death of their father.

They are the only two sisters now living of the Campbell family.

3. Dennis is the third member of our family. He is a free man in Kentucky, and is doing a very good business there. He was assisted by a Mr. William L. Stevenson, and also by his sister, in getting his freedom. He never had any knowledge of our intention of running away, nor did he assist us in any manner whatever.

4. Alexander is the fourth child of my mother. He is the slave of a Dr. Richardson; has with him a very easy time; lives as well as a man can and be a slave; has no intention of running away. He lives very much like a second-hand gentleman, and I do not know as he would leave Kentucky on any condition.

5. My mother lost her fifth child soon after it was born.

6. Delia came next. Hers was a most bitter and tragical history. She was so unfortunate as to be uncommonly handsome,

and, when arrived at woman's estate, was considered a great prize for the guilty passions of the slaveholders.

7. To No. 7 I, Lewis Clarke, respond, and of me you have heard enough already.

8. Milton comes next, and he is speaking for himself. He is almost constantly engaged in giving lectures upon the subject of slavery; has more calls usually than he can attend to.

9. Manda, the ninth child, died when she was about fifteen or sixteen years of age. She suffered a good deal from Joseph Logan's second wife.

10. Cyrus is the youngest of the family, and lives at Hamilton, New York.

QUESTIONS AND ANSWERS.

BY LEWIS CLARKE.

THE following questions are often asked me, when I meet the people in public, and I have thought it would be well to put down the answers here.

How many holidays in a year do the slaves in Kentucky have?--They usually have six days at Christmas, and two or three others in the course of the year. Public opinion generally seems to require this much of slaveholders; a few give more, some less; some none, not a day nor an hour.

How do slaves spend the Sabbath?--Every way the master pleases. There are certain kinds of work which are respectable for Sabbath day. Slaves are often sent out to salt the cattle, collect and count the pigs and sheep, mend fences, drive the stock from one pasture to another. Breaking young horses and mules, to send them to market, yoking young oxen, and training them, is proper Sabbath work; piling and burning brush, on the back part of the lot, grubbing brier patches that are out of the way, and where they will not be seen. Sometimes corn must be shelled in the corn-crib; hemp is baled in the hemp-house. The still-house must be attended on the Sabbath. In these, and various other such like employments, the more avaricious slaveholders keep their slaves busy a good part of every Sabbath. It is a great day for visiting and eating, and the house servants often have more to do on that than on any other day.

What if strangers come along, and see you at work?--We must quit shelling corn, and go to play with the cobs; or else we must be clearing land, on our own account. We must cover up master's sins as much as possible, and take it all to ourselves. It is hardly fair; for he ought rather to account for our sins, than we for his.

Why did you not learn to read?--I did not dare to learn. I attempted to spell some words when a child. One of the children of Mrs. Banton went in, and told her that she heard Lewis spelling. Mrs. B. jumped up as though she had been shot. "Let me ever know you to spell another word, I'll take your heart right out of you." I had a strong desire to learn. But it would not do to have slaves learn to read and write. They could read the guide-boards. They could write passes for each other. They cannot leave the plantation on the Sabbath without a written pass.

What proportion of slaves attend church on the Sabbath?--In the country, not more than one in ten on an average.

How many slaves have you ever known that could read?--I never saw more than three or four that could properly read at all. I never saw but one that could write.

What do slaves know about the Bible?--They generally believe there is somewhere a real Bible, that came from God; but they frequently say the Bible now used is master's Bible; most that they hear from it being, "Servants, obey your masters."

Are families often separated? How many such cases have you personally known?--I never knew a whole family to live together till all were grown up, in my life. There is almost always, in every family, some one or more keen and bright, or else sullen and stubborn slave, whose influence they are afraid of on the rest or the family, and such a one must take a walking ticket to the south.

There are other causes of separation. The death of a large owner is the occasion usually of many families being broken up. Bankruptcy is another cause of separation, and the hard-heartedness of a majority of slaveholders another and a more fruitful cause than either or all the rest. Generally there is but little more scruple about separating families than there is with a man who keeps sheep in selling off the lambs in the fall. On one plantation where I lived, there was an old slave named Paris. He was from fifty to sixty years old, and a very honest and apparently pious slave. A slave-trader came along one day, gathering hands for the south. The old master ordered the waiter or coachman to take Paris into the back room, pluck out all his gray hairs, rub his face with a greasy towel, and then had him brought forward and sold for a young man. His wife consented to go with him, upon a promise from the trader that they should be sold together, with their youngest child, which she carried in her arms. They left two behind them, who were only from four to six or eight years of age. The speculator collected his drove, started for the market, and, before he left the state, he sold that infant child to pay one of his tavern bills, and took the balance in cash. This was the news which came back to us, and was never disputed.

I saw one slave mother, named Lucy, with seven children, put up by an administrator for sale. At first the mother and three small children were put up together. The purchasers objected: one says, "I want the woman and the babe, but not the other children;" another says, "I want that little girl;" and another, "I want the boy."

"Well," says the administrator, "I must let you have them to the best advantage." So the children were taken away; the mother and infant were first sold, then child after child-- the mother looking on in perfect agony; and as one child after another came down from the auction block, they would run and cling, weeping, to her clothes. The poor mother stood, till nature gave way; she fainted and fell, with her child in her arms. The only sympathy she received from most of the hard-hearted monsters, who had riven he heart-strings asunder, was, "She is a d--d deceitful bitch; I wish she was mine; I would teach her better than to cut up such shines as that here." When she came to, she moaned wofully, and prayed that she might die, to be relieved from her sufferings.

I knew another slave, named Nathan, who had a slave woman for a wife. She was killed by hard usage. Nathan then declared he would never have another slave wife. He selected a free woman for a companion. His master opposed it violently. But Nathan persevered in his choice, and in consequence was sold to go down south. He returned once to see his wife, and she soon after died of grief and disappointment. On his return south, he leaped from the boat, and attempted to swim ashore; his master, on board the boat, took a gun and deliberately shot him, and he drifted down the current of the river.

On this subject of separation of families, I must plant one more rose in the garland that I have already tied upon the brow of the sweet Mrs. Banton. The reader cannot have forgotten her; and in the delectable business of tearing families asunder, she, of course, would have a hand. A slave by the name of Susan was taken by Mrs. Banton on mortgage. She had been well treated where she was brought up, had a husband, and they were very happy together. Susan mourned in bitterness over her separation, and pined away under the cruel hand of Mrs. Banton. At length she ran away, and hid herself in the neighborhood of her husband. When this came to the knowledge of Mrs. B., she charged her husband to go for "Suke," and never let her see his face unless she was with him. "No," said she, "if you are offered a double price, don't you take it. I want my satisfaction out of her, and then you may sell her as soon as you please." Susan was brought back in fetters, and Mr. and Mrs. B. both took their satisfaction; they beat and tortured poor Susan till her premature offspring perished, and she almost sank beneath their merciless hands, and then they sold her to be carried a hundred miles farther away from her husband. Ah! slavery is like running the dissecting knife around the heart, among all the tender fibres of our being.

A man by the name of Bill Myers, in Kentucky, went to a large number of auctions, and purchased women about forty years old, with their youngest children in their arms. As they are about to cease bearing at that age, they are sold cheap. The children he took and shut up in a log pen, and set some old worn-out slave women to make broth and feed them. The mothers be gathered in a large drove, and carried them south and sold them. He was detained there for months longer than he expected; and, winter coming on, and no proper provision having been made for the children, many of them perished with cold and hunger, some were frostbitten, and all were emaciated to skeletons. This was the only attempt that I ever knew for gathering young children together, like a litter of pigs, to be raised for the market. The success was not such as to warrant a repetition on the part of Myers.

Jockey Billy Barnett had a slave-prison, where he gathered his droves of husbands, fathers, and wives, separated from their friends: and he tried to keep up their spirits by employing one or two fiddlers to play for them, while they danced over and upon the torn-off fibres of their hearts. Several women were known to have died in that worse than Calcutta Black Hole of grief. They mourned for their children, and would not be comforted, because they were not.

How are the slave cabins usually built?--They are made of small logs, about from ten to twenty feet square. The roof is covered with splits, and dirt is thrown in to raise the bottom, and then it is beat down hard for a floor. The chimneys are made of cut sticks and clay. In the corners, or at the sides, there are pens made, filled with straw, for sleeping. Very commonly, two or three families are huddled together in one cabin, and in cold weather they sleep together promiscuously, old and young. Some few families are indulged in the privilege of having a few hens or ducks around them; but this is not very common.

What amount of food do slaves have in Kentucky?--They are not put on allowance; they generally have enough of corn bread; and meat and soup are dealt to them occasionally.

What is the clothing of a slave for a year?-- For summer, he has usually a pair of tow and linen pants, and two shirts of the same material. He has a pair of shoes, a pair of woolsey pants, and a round jacket for winter.

The account current of a slave with his master stands about thus:--

ICHABOD LIVE-WITHOUT-WORK, in account with JOHN WORK-WITHOUT-PAY.

- Dr.
  To one man's work, one year, ... $100 00
- Contra, Cr.
  By 13 bushels of corn meal, at 10 cents, ... $1 30
- " 100 lbs. mean bacon and pork, at 1 1/2 cents, ... 1 50
- " Chickens, pigs, &c., taken without leave, say 1 50
- " 9 yds. of tow and linen, for shirts and pants, at 12 1/2 cents 1 12 1/2
- " 1 pair of shoes, ... 1 50
- " Cloth for jacket and winter pants, 5 1/2 yds., at 2 shillings, ... 1 84
- " Making clothes 1 00
- " 1 Blanket, ... 1 00
- " 2 Hats or caps, ... 75
- [Total]--$ 11 51 1/2
- Balance due the slave every year $88 48 1/2

The account stands unbalanced thus till the great day of reckoning comes.

Now, allow that one half of the slaves are capable of labor; that they can earn, on an average, one half the sum above named; that would give us $50 a year for 1,500,000 slaves, which would be seventy-five millions as the sum robbed from the slaves every year!! "Woe unto him that useth his neighbor's service without wages!" Woe unto him that buildeth his house by iniquity, "for the stone shall cry out of the wall, and the beam out of the timber shall answer it!" "Behold, the hire of the laborers, who have reaped down your fields, which is of you kept back by fraud, crieth; and the cries of them which have reaped are entered into the ears of the Lord of Sabaoth. Ye have lived in pleasure on the earth, and been wanton; ye have nourished your hearts, as in a day of slaughter."

Have you ever known a slave mother to kill her own children?--There was a slave mother near where I lived, who took her child into the cellar and killed it. She did it to prevent being separated from her child. Another slave mother took her three children and threw them into a well, and then jumped in with them, and they were all drowned. Other instances I have frequently heard of. At the death of many and many a slave child, I have seen the two feelings struggling in the bosom of a mother-- joy, that it was beyond the reach of the slave monsters, and the natural grief of a mother over her child. In the presence of the master, grief seems to predominate; when away from them, they rejoice that there is one whom the slave-driver will never torment.

How is it that masters KILL their slaves, when they are worth so much money?--They do it to gratify passion; this must be done, cost what it may. Some say a man will not kill a horse worth a hundred dollars, much less a slave worth several hundred dollars. A horse has no such will of his own, as the slave has; he does not provoke the man, as a slave does. The master knows there is contrivance with the slave to outwit him; the horse has no such contrivance. This conflict of the two WILLS is what makes the master so much more passionate with his slave than with a horse. A slaveholder must be master on the plantation, or he knows the example would destroy all authority.

What do they do with old slaves, who are past labor?--Contrive all ways to keep them at work till the last hour of life. Make them shell corn and pack tobacco. They hunt and drive them as long as there is any life in them. Sometimes they turn them out to do the best they can, or die. One man, on moving to Missouri, sold an old slave for one dollar, to a man not worth a cent. The old slave was turned out to do the best he could; he fought with age and starvation a while, but was soon found, one morning, starved to death, out of doors, and half eaten up by animals. I have known several cases where slaves were left to starve to death in old age. Generally, they sell them south, and let them die there; send them, I mean, before they get very old.

What makes them wash slaves in salt and water after they whip them?--For two reasons; one is to make them smart, and another to prevent mortification in the lacerated flesh. I have seen men and women both washed after they had been cruelly beaten. I have done it with my own hands. It was the hardest work I ever did. The flesh would crawl, and creep, and quiver, under my hands. This slave's name was Tom. He had not started his team Sunday morning early enough. The neighbors saw that Mr. Banton had work done on the Sabbath. Dalton, the overseer, attempted to whip him. Tom knocked him down and trod on him, and then ran away. The patrols caught him, and he was whipped--three hundred lashes. Such a back I never saw; such work I pray that I may never do again.

Do not slaves often say that they love their masters very much?--Say so? yes, certainly. And this loving master and mistress is the hardest work that slaves have to do. When any stranger is present, we have to love them very much. When master is sick, we are in great trouble. Every night the slaves gather around the house, and send up one or two to see how master does. They creep up to the bed, and with a very soft voice, inquire, "How is dear massa? O massa, how we want to hear your voice out in the field again!" Well, this is what they say up in the sick room. They come down to their anxious companions. "How is the old man?" "Will he die?" "Yes, yes; he sure to go, this time; he never whip the slave no more." "Are you sure? Will he die?" "O yes! surely gone for it, now." Then they all look glad, and go to the cabin with a merry heart.

Two slaves were sent out to dig a grave for old master. They dug it very deep. As I passed by, I asked Jess and Bob what in the world they dug it so deep for. It was down six or seven feet. I told them there would be a fuss about it, and they had better fill it up some. Jess said it suited him exactly. Bob said he would not fill it up; he wanted to get the old man as near home as possible. When we got a stone to put on his grave, we hauled the largest we could find, so as to fasten him down as strong as possible.

Another story illustrates the feeling of the slaves on taking leave of their masters. I will not vouch for the truth of it; but it is a story slaves delight to tell each other. The master called the slave to his sick bed. "Good-by, Jack; I have a long journey to go; farewell." "Farewell, massa! pleasant journey: you soon be dere, massa--all de way downhill!"

Who are the patrols?--They are men appointed by the county courts to look after all slaves without a pass. They have almost unlimited power over the slaves. They are the sons of run-down families. The greatest scoundrel is always captain of the band of patrols. They are the offscouring of all things; the refuse, the fag end, the ears and tails of slavery; the scales and fins of fish; the tooth and tongues of serpents. They are the very fool's cap of baboons, the echo of parrots, the wallet and satchel of polecats, the scum of stagnant pools, the exuvial, the worn-out skins of slaveholders; they dress in their old clothes. They are, emphatically, the servants of servants, and slaves of the devil; they are the meanest, and lowest, and worst of all creation. Like starved wharf rats, they are out nights, creeping into slave cabins, to see if they have an old bone there; drive out husbands from their own beds, and then take their places. They get up all sorts of pretences, false as their lying tongues can make them, and then whip the slaves and carry a gory lash to the master, for a piece of bread.

The rascals run me with their dogs six miles, one night, and I was never nearer dead than when I reached home that night. I only escaped being half torn to pieces by the dogs, by turning their attention to some calves that were in the road. The dogs are so trained that they will seize a man as quick as any thing else. The dogs come very near being as mean as their masters.

Cyrus often suffered very much from these wretches. He was hired with a man named Baird. This man was reputed to be very good to his slaves. The patrols, therefore, had a special spite toward his slaves. They would seek for an opportunity to abuse them. Mr. Baird would generally give his slaves a pass to go to the neighbors, once or twice a week, if requested. He had been very good to Cyrus in this respect, and therefore Cyrus was unwilling to ask too often. Once he went out without his pass. The patrols found him and some other slaves on another plantation without any passes. The other slaves belonged to a plantation where they were often whipped; so they gave them a moderate punishment and sent them home. Cyrus, they said, they would take to the woods, and have a regular whipping spree. It was a cold winter night, the moon shining brightly. When they had got into the woods, they ordered him to take off his outside coat, then his jacket; then he said he had a new vest on; he did not want that whipped all to pieces. There were seven men standing in a ring around him. He looked for an opening, and started at full speed. They took after him, but he was too spry for them.

He came to the cabin where I slept, and I lent him a hat and a pair of shoes. He was very much excited; said they were all around him, but couldn't whip him. He went over to Mr. Baird, and the patrols had got there before him, and had brought his clothes and told their story. It was now eight or nine o'clock in the evening. Mr. Baird, when a young man, had lived on the plantation of Mr. Logan, and had been treated very kindly by mother. He remembered this kindness to her children. When Cyrus came in, Mr. Baird took his clothes and handed them to him, and told him, "Well, boy, they came pretty near catching you." Cyrus put on his clothes, went into the room where the patrols were, and said, "Good evening, gentlemen. Why, I did not think the patrols would be out to-night. I was thinking of going over to Mr. Reed's; if I had, I should have gone without a pass. They would have caught me, sure enough. Mr. Baird, I wish you would be good enough to give me a pass, and then I won't be afraid of these fellows." Mr. Baird enjoyed the fun right well, and sat down and wrote him a pass; and the patrols started, and had to find the money for their peach brandy somewhere else.

There were several other times when he had but a hair-breadth escape for his skin. He was generally a little too shrewd for them. After he had outwitted them several times, they offered a premium to any one who would whip him.

How do slaves get information of what is doing in the free states?--In different ways. They get something from the waiters, that come out into the free states and then return with their masters. Persons from the free states tell them many things; the free blacks get something; and slaves learn most of all from hearing their masters talk.

Don't slaves that run away return sometimes?-- Yes; there was one returned from Canada, very sorry he had run away. His master was delighted with him; thought he had him sure for life, and made much of him. He was sent round to tell how bad Canada was. He had a sermon for the public,-- the ear of the masters,--and another for the slaves. How many he enlightened about the best way to get there, I don't know. His master, at last, was so sure of him, that he let him take his wife and children and go over to Ohio, to a camp-meeting, all fitted out in good style, with horse and wagon. They never stopped to hear any preaching, till they heard the waves of the lakes lift up their cheerful voices between them and the oppressor. George then wrote an affectionate note to his master, inviting him to take tea with him in Canada, beyond the waters, the barrier of freedom. Whether the old people ever went up to Canada, to see their affectionate children, I have not learned. I have heard of several instances very much like the above.

If the slaves were set free, would they cut the throats of their masters?--They are far more likely to kill them, if they don't set them free. Nothing but the hope of emancipation, and the fear they might not succeed, keeps them from rising to assert their rights. They are restrained, also, from affection for the children of those who so cruelly oppress them. If none would suffer but the masters themselves, the slaves would make many more efforts for freedom. And, sooner or later, unless the slaves are given free, they will take freedom, at all hazards. There are multitudes that chafe under the yoke, sorely enough. They could run away themselves, but they would hate to leave their families.

Did the slaves in Kentucky hear of the emancipation in the West Indies?--They did, in a very short time after it took place. It was the occasion of great joy. They expected they would be free next. This event has done much to keep up the hopes of the slave to the present hour.

What do slaves think of the PIETY of their masters?--They have very little confidence in them about any thing. As a specimen of their feelings on this subject, I will tell an anecdote of a slave.

A slave, named George, was the property of a man of high standing in the church. The old gentleman was taken sick, and the doctor told him he would die. He called George, and told him if he would wait upon him attentively, and do every thing for him possible, he would remember him in his will: he would do something handsome for him.

George was very much excited to know what it might be; hoped it might be in the heart of his master to give him his freedom. At last, the will was made. George was still more excited. The master noticed it, and asked what the matter was. "Massa, you promise do something for me in your will. Poor nigger! what massa done for George?" "O George, don't be concerned; I have done a very handsome thing for you--such as any slave would be proud to have done for him." This did not satisfy George. He was still very eager to know what it was. At length the master saw it necessary to tell George, to keep him quiet, and make him attend to his duty. "Well, George, I have made provision that, when you die, you shall have a good coffin, and be put into the same vault with me. Will not that satisfy you, George?"

"Well, massa, one way I am satisfied, and one way I am not." "What, what," said the old master, "what is the matter with that?" "Why," says George, "I like to have good coffin when I die." "Well, don't you like to be in the same vault with me and other rich masters?" "Why, yes, massa, one way I like it, and one way I don't." "Well, what don't you like?" "Why, I fraid, massa, when de debbil come take you body, he make mistake, and get mine."

The slaves uniformly prefer to be buried at the greatest possible distance away from master. They are superstitious, and fear that the slave-driver, having whipped so much when alive, will, somehow, be beating them when dead. I was actually as much afraid of my old master when dead, as I was when he was alive. I often dreamed of him, too, after he was dead, and thought he had actually come back again, to torment me more.

Do slaves have conscientious scruples about taking things from their masters?-- They think it wrong to take from a neighbor, but not from their masters. The only question with them is, "Can we keep it from master?" If they can keep their backs safe, conscience is quiet enough on this point. But a slave that will steal from a slave, is called mean as master. This is the lowest comparison slaves know how to use: "just as mean as white folks." "No right for to complain of white folks, who steal us all de days of our life; nigger dat what steal from nigger, be meaner nor all."

There is no standard of morality in the slave states. The master stands before the slave a robber and oppressor. His words count nothing with the slaves. The slaves are disrobed of the attributes of men, so that they cannot hold up the right standard, and there is none. The slaves frequently have discussions upon moral questions. Sol and Tom went, one night, to steal the chickens of a neighbor. Tom went up, to hand them down to Sol. While engaged in this operation, he paused a minute. "Sol, you tink dis right, to steal dese chicken from here?" "What dat you say, Tom?" "I say, you tink him right to steal dese chicken, Sol?" "What you come talk dat way, now, for? Dat quession you ought settle 'fore you come here." "Me did tink about it, but want to hear what you say, Sol. Don't you tink it kind of wrong to take dese here chicken?" "I tell you, Sol, no time for 'scuss dat now. Dat is de great moral question. Make haste; hand me down anudder one; let us git away from here 'fore de daylight come."

Do you think it was right for you to run away, and not pay any thing for yourself?--I would be willing to pay, if I knew who to pay it to. But when I think it over, I can't find any body that has any better right to me than myself. I can't pay father and mother, for they are dead. I don't owe Mrs. Banton any thing for bringing me up the way she did. I worked five or six years, and earned more than one hundred dollars a year, for Mr. K. and family, and received about a dozen dollars a year in clothing. Who do I owe, then, in Kentucky? If I catch one of the administrators on here, I intend to sue him for wages, and interest, for six years' hard work. There will be a small bill of damages for abuse; old Kentucky is not rich enough to pay me for that.

Soon after you came into Ohio, did you let yourself to work?--I did,--Was there any difference in your feelings while laboring there, and as a slave in Kentucky?--I made a bargain to work for a man in Ohio. I took a job of digging a cellar. Before I began, the people told me he was bad pay; they would not do it for him. I told them I had agreed to do it. So at it I went, worked hard, and got it off as soon as possible, although I did not expect to get a cent for it; and yet I worked more readily, and with a better mind, than I ever did in Kentucky. If I worked for nothing then, I knew I had made my own bargain; and working with that thought made it easier than any day's work I ever did for a master in Kentucky. That thought was worth more than any pay I ever got in slavery. However, I was more fortunate than many thought I should be; through the exertions of a good friend, I got my pay soon after the work was done.

Why do slaves dread so bad to go to the south-- to Mississippi or Louisiana?--Because they know that slaves are driven very hard there, and worked to death in a few years.

Are those who have GOOD masters afraid of being sold south?--They all suffer very much for fear master's circumstances will change, and that he may be compelled to sell them to the "SOUL-DRIVERS," a name given to the dealers by the slaves.

What is the highest price you ever knew a slave to sell for?--I have known a man sold for $1465. He was a waiter-man, very intelligent, very humble, and a good house servant. A good blacksmith, as I was told, was once sold in Kentucky for $3000. I have heard of handsome girls being sold in New Orleans for from $2000 to $3000. The common price of females is about from $500 to $700, when sold for plantation hands, for house hands, or for breeders.

Why is a black slave-driver worse than a white one?--He must be very strict and severe, or else he will be turned out. The master selects the hardest-hearted and most unprincipled slave upon the plantation. The overseers are usually a part of the patrols. Which is the worst of the two characters, or officers, is hard to tell.

Are the masters afraid of insurrection?--They live in constant and great fear upon this subject. The least unusual noise at night alarms them greatly. They cry out, "What is that?" "Are the boys all in?"

What is the worst thing you ever saw in Kentucky?--The worst thing I ever saw was a woman, stripped all naked, hung up by her hands, and then whipped till the blood ran down her back. Sometimes this is done by a young master, or mistress, to aged mother, or even a grandmother. Nothing the slaves abhor as they do this.

Which is the worst, a master or a mistress?--A mistress is far worse. She is forever and ever tormenting. When the master whips it is done with; but a mistress will blackguard, scold, and tease, and whip the life out of a slave.

How soon do the children begin to exercise their authority?--From the very breast of the mother. I have seen a child, before he could talk a word, have a stick put into his hand, and he was permitted to whip a slave, in order to quiet him. And from the time they are born till they die, they live by whipping and abusing the slave.

Do you suffer from cold in Kentucky?--Many people think it so warm there that we are safe on this score. They are much mistaken. The weather is far too cold for our thin clothing; and in winter, from rain, sleet, and snow, to which we are exposed, we suffer very severely. Such a thing as a greatcoat the slave very seldom has.

What do they raise in Kentucky?--Corn and hemp, tobacco, oats, some wheat and rye; SLAVES, mules, hogs, and horses, for the southern market.

Do the masters drink a great deal?-- They are nearly all hard drinkers--many of them drunkards; and you must not exclude mistress from the honor of drinking, as she is often drunk, too.

Are you not afraid they will send up and catch you, and carry you back to Kentucky?--They may make the attempt; but I made up my mind, when I left slavery, never to go back there and continue alive. I fancy I should be a load for one or two of them to carry back, any how. Besides, they well know that they could not take me out of any state this side of Pennsylvania. There are very few in New England that would sell themselves to help a slaveholder; and if they should, they would have to run their country. They would be hooted at as they walked the streets.

Now, in conclusion, I just want to say, that all the abuses which I have here related are necessary, if slavery must continue to exist. It is impossible to out off these abuses and keep slavery alive. Now, if you do not approve of these horrid sufferings, I entreat you to lift up your voice and your hand against the whole system, and, with one united effort, overturn the abominations of centuries, and restore scattered families to each other; pour light upon millions of dark minds, and make a thousand, yea, ten times ten thousand, abodes of wretchedness and woe to hail and bless you as angels of mercy sent for their deliverance.

FACTS FROM THE PERSONAL KNOWLEDGE OF MILTON CLARKE.

GENERAL LESLIE COOMBS, of Lexington, owned a man named Ennis, a house carpenter. He had bargained with a slave-trader to take him and carry him down the river. Ennis was determined not to go. He took a broad-axe and cut one hand off; then contrived to lift the axe, with his arm pressing it to his body, and let it fall upon the other, cutting off the ends of his fingers. His master sold him for a nominal price, and down he went to Louisiana.

A slave named Jess, belonging to Deacon Logan, went out one Sabbath evening for the same purpose that many young men have for making calls on that evening. Jack White, a captain of the patrols, followed Jess, and took him out and whipped him, in the presence of the family where Jess was making his call. The indignation of poor Jess was roused. He sought his way by stealthy steps, at night, to the barn of Jack

White, and touched it with the match. Jess was suspected, and his master told him, if guilty, he had better own it, and he would send him down the river to save him from being hung. Jess was put in jail on suspicion[.] Deacon Logan sent his slaves by night; they got Jess out of jail; he was concealed by his master for a few days, and then sold for $700, and sent down the river.

HIRED SLAVES.--BAGGING FACTORIES.

In and around Lexington are numerous factories for spinning and weaving hemp bagging. Young slaves, from ten to fifteen years old, are employed in spinning. They are hired for $20 to $30 a year, and their condition is a very hard and cruel one. They have a weekly task. So much hemp is weighed out; so much filling must be returned, all of the right size, and at the proper time. Want of skill, mistakes of various kinds, subject them to frequent and unmerited stripes.

An overseer of one of these factories, Tom Monks, would tie up his poor boys, and give them from forty to fifty hashes. He kept them sometimes yoked with iron collars, with prongs sticking out, and the name of the owner written on them. Working in these factories takes all the life and spirit out of a young slave, and he soon becomes little better than an idiot. This is the worst kind of slavery in Kentucky. When the life is thus taken out of these poor lads, at the age of eighteen or twenty, they are sold for Louisiana. Here a short but bitter doom awaits them.

They are first carried to New Orleans, and put in pens. When a purchaser comes and inquires of the slave what he can do, he must make pretensions, of course, to great skill and ability, or the seller will abuse him. But what will be his condition with the purchaser, who finds that he cannot do half the things he promised? The sugar-planter blames the slave. He came from the bag factory, but said he was a good field hand; could hold plough, hoe corn, or any other kind of farming work in Kentucky. He has lied to his present master, for the benefit of his former one. He atones for it by many a cruel flogging. When they find one that is very awkward and ignorant, the master tells the overseer to "put him through for what be is worth;" "use him up as soon as you can;" "get what you can out of him in a short time, and let him die." In a few years, the poor fellow ends his labors and his sorrows.

The bell rings at four o'clock in the morning, and they have half an hour to get ready. Men and women start together, and the women must work as steadily as the men, and perform the same tasks as the men. If the plantation is far from the house, the sucking children are taken out and kept in the field all day. If the cabins are near, the women are permitted to go in two or three times a day to their infant children. The mother is driven out when the child is three to four weeks old. The dews of the morning are very heavy, and wet the slaves all through. Many, from the upper slave states, die from change of climate and diet. At the time of making sugar and molasses, the slaves are kept up half the night; and the worst-looking creatures I ever saw were the slaves that make the sugar for those sensitive ladies and gentlemen, who cannot bear the sight of a colored person, but who are compelled to use the sugar made by the filthiest class of slaves.

O, how would LIBERTY wash away the filth and the misery of millions! Then the slaves would be washed, and clothed, and fed, and instructed, and made happy!

There is another and very different class of slaves sent south. When a body servant refuses to be whipped, or his master breaks with him for any other reason, he is sold south. The purchaser questions him, and he tells the truth. "Can you farm?" "No, sir." "What can you do?" "Work in garden, drive horses, and work around the house." "Ay; gentleman nigger, are you? Well, you are gentleman nigger no longer." He is ordered upon the plantation, and soon acquires skill to perform his task. Always sure to perform all that is required, he does not intend to be beaten by any human being. The overseer soon discovers this spirit, and seeks occasion for a quarrel. The slave will not be whipped. A half a dozen overseers are called together, and the poor fellow is chained, and whipped to the border of his grave. In a week or two, the overseer tries his spirit again; comes into the field and strikes him, by way of insult, and the slave knocks him down, and perhaps kills him with his hoe, and flies for the woods, Then horses, dogs, overseers, planters, lawyers, doctors, ministers, are all summoned out on a grand nigger hunt, and poor Bill Turner is shot dead at the foot of a tree, and the trumpet sounds at once a triumph and a retreat.

I expect nothing but there may be an attempt made to carry me back to slavery: but I give fair warning to all concerned, that now, knowing the value of liberty, I prize it far above life; and no year of suns will ever shine upon my chains as a slave. I can die, but I cannot be made a slave again. Lewis says, "Amen! Brother Milton, give me your hand! You speak my mind exactly."

CALLING ON THEIR MASTERS FOR HELP.

THE Frankfort (Ky.) "Commonwealth" publishes a rich letter from the Ohio justice of the peace, who assisted the kidnappers of Jerry Phinney. It is addressed to the person who now has possession of Jerry, and calls lustily on him to save the wretched justice from the penitentiary. He, and the man who taught him that "that is property which the law declares to be property," ought both to go to the penitentiary till they can unlearn that diabolical sophism. The fellow really talks as though it made a vast difference in his crime, whether the victim had been entangled in a similar manner before. He writes,--

"I wish you, as a friend, to ascertain if the power of attorney, presented to me by said Forbes, is a lawful and true one, and if the said Jerry Phinney is a slave or not; for if he is not, it will go very hard with us, and is a perjury on the said Forbes, in consequence of the affidavit he filed with me.

"And to you, Kentuckians, I appeal for redress for the severe treatment we have received, in consequence of the seizure and conveying off of a slave, as I verily and solemnly believe Jerry; for I cannot for one moment believe that said power of attorney is a forgery, and that Forbes committed perjury.

"And we earnestly solicit your aid; for, without, the state prison is our doom; although I acted in good faith.

"The abolitionists are determined that we shall be convicted of kidnapping.

"We are very poor, but defy the world to bring a dishonorable act against us, except the one now against us, which they deem a great one; but I deny being guilty of any such charge.

"Unless you aid and assist us, you may rely on it that you never need expect an officer, in this section of the country, ever again to touch any thing of the kind, for fear of the penitentiary; for prejudice and abolitionism are bent to imprison any justice of the peace, who dare make an attempt to examine a fugitive from labor, and more particularly if he is poor, and has not money to carry him through a course of law.

"Prejudice is so great, that I am credibly informed the governor has issued his proclamation, offering a reward of one thousand dollars for the apprehension of said Forbes, and Jacob Armatage, the young man that went with Forbes; the citizens are to pay half of said reward.

"Please favor me with an immediate answer; and inform me what proof can be had that Jerry is a slave, and what relief can be rendered us in our distressing case. You may also look for a letter from our attorneys, F. J. Mathews and Colonel N. H. Swayne, as they will address all those whose signatures are in said power of attorney, which is in their hands at this time; and that is the reason I have not given their Christian names.

"WM. HENDERSON, J. P.

"H. D. HENDERSON.

"D. A. POTTER."

PRESIDENT EDWARDS.--A TESTIMONY.

ON the 15th of September, 1791, the younger Edwards, then pastor of a church in New Haven, preached a sermon before the Connecticut Society for the Promotion of Freedom, &c., in which he has the following remarks:--

"The arguments which have been urged against the slave-trade, are, with little variation, applicable to the holding of slaves. He who holds a slave, continues to deprive him of that liberty which was taken from him on the coast of Africa. And if it were wrong to deprive him of it in the first instance, why not in the second? If this be true, no man has a better right to retain his negro in slavery, than he had to take him from his native African shores. And every man who cannot show that his negro hath, by his voluntary conduct, forfeited his liberty, is obliged immediately to manumit him.

"I presume it will not be denied that to commit theft or robbery every day of a man's life, is as great a sin as to commit fornication in one instance. But to steal a MAN, or to rob him of his liberty, is a greater sin than to steal his property, or to take it by violence. And to hold a man in a state of slavery, who has a right to his liberty, is to be every day guilty of robbing him of his liberty, or of man-stealing. The consequence is inevitable, that, other things being the same, to hold a negro slave, unless he has forfeited his liberty, is a greater sin than concubinage and fornication.

"To convince yourselves that, your information being the same, to hold a negro slave is a greater sin than fornication, theft, or robbery, you need only bring the matter home to yourselves. I am willing to appeal to your own consciousness, whether you would not judge it to be a greatest sin for a man to hold you or your children, during life, in such slavery as that of the negroes, than for him to indulge in one instance of licentious conduct, or in one instance to steal or rob. Let conscience speak, and I will submit to its decision."

If the above remarks were correct in 1791, can they be wrong in 1846? If our good divines were correct in calling slaveholders man-stealers, and slaveholding a greater sin in the sight of God than concubinage and fornication, what must we think of the moral state or the heart of those modern D. D.'s, who are willing to receive slaveholders into the church of God, and are ready to weave out of their own hearts a theological fiction to palliate the enormous evil? Alas! C. M. Clay is right, when he says, "The disease is of the heart, and not of the head. We tell you, brothers, that the American people know well enough that the bloody stain is upon them--but they love its taint! If we can't arouse the conscience, and ennoble the heart, our labor is lost. A seared conscience and a heart hardened by sin--these are the grand supporters of slavery in and out of the church. How can these giants be subdued?--From the Charter Oak.

ORDER OF EXERCISES FOR A SLAVEHOLDERS' MEETING.

I. PRAYER.

BY CASSIUS M. CLAY.

Prayer and Slavery.

THERE are many men, professing the Christian religion, who also profess to believe slavery a divine institution! Now, we have lived thus long, and never yet have heard a prayer offered up to God in its behalf! If it is of God, Christians, pray for it! Try it; it will strengthen your faith and purify your souls.

O THOU omnipotent and benevolent God, who hast made all men of one flesh, thou Father of all nations, we do most devoutly beseech thee to defend and strengthen thy institution, American slavery! Do thou, O Lord, tighten the chains of our black brethren, and cause slavery to increase and multiply throughout the world! And whereas many nations of the earth have loved their neighbors as themselves, and have done unto others as they would that others should do unto them, and have broken every bond, and have let the oppressed go free, do thou, O God, turn their hearts from their evil ways, and let them seize once more upon the weak and defenceless, and subject them to eternal servitude!

And, O God, as thou hast commanded us not to muzzle even the poor ox that treadeth out the corn, let them labor unceasingly without reward, and let their own husbands, and wives, and children, be sold into distant lands without crime, that thy name may be glorified, and that unbelievers may be confounded, and forced to confess that indeed thou art a God of justice and mercy! Stop, stop, O God, the escape from the prison-house, by which thousands of these "accursed" men flee into foreign countries, where nothing but tyranny reigns; and compel them to enjoy the unequalled blessings of our own free land!

Whereas our rulers in the Alabama legislature have emancipated a black man, because of some eminent public service, thus bringing thy holy name into shame, do thou, O God, change their hearts, melt them into mercy, and into obedience to thy will, and cause them speedily to restore the chain to that unfortunate soul! And, O God, thou Searcher of all hearts, seeing that many of thine own professed followers, when they come to lie down on the bed of death, and enter upon that bourn whence no traveller returns,--where every one shall be called to account for the deeds done in the body, whether they be good or whether they be evil,--emancipate their fellow-men, failing in faith, and given over to hardness of heart and blindness of perception of the truth, do thou, O God, be merciful to them and the poor recipients of their deceitful philanthropy, and let the chain enter into the flesh and the iron into the soul forever!

II. HYMN.

PARODY.

COME, saints and sinners, hear me tell
How pious priests whip Jack and Nell,
And women buy, and children sell,
And preach all sinners down to hell,
And sing of heavenly union.

They'll bleat and baa, dona like goats,
Gorge down black sheep, and strain at motes,
Array their backs in fine black coats,
And seize their negroes by their throats,
And choke, for heavenly union.

They'll church you if you sip a dram,
And damn you if you steal a lamb;
Yet rob old Tony, Doll, and Sam,
Of human rights, and bread and ham--
Kidnapper's heavenly union.

They'll talk of heaven and Christ's reward,
And bind his image with a cord,
And scold and swing the lash abhorred,
And sell their brother in the Lord
To handcuffed heavenly union.

They'll read and sing a sacred song,
And make a prayer both loud and long,
And teach the right and do the wrong;

Hailing the brother, sister throng,
With words of heavenly union.

We wonder how such saints can sing,
Or praise the Lord upon the wing,
Who roar and scold, and whip and sting,
And to their slaves and mammon cling,
In guilty conscience union.

They'll raise tobacco, corn, and rye,
And drive and thieve, and cheat and lie,
And lay up treasures in the sky,

By making switch and cowskin fly,
In hope of heavenly union.

They'll crack old Tony on the skull,
And preach and roar like Bashan bull,
Or braying ass of mischief full;
Then seize old Jacob by the wool,
And pull for heavenly union.

A roaring, ranting, sleek man-thief,
Who lived on mutton, veal, and beef,
And never would afford relief
To needy sable sons of grief,
Was big with heavenly union.

Love not the world, the preacher said,
And winked his eye and shook his head;--
He seized on Tom, and Dick, and Ned,
Cut short their meat, and clothes, and bread,
Yet still loved heavenly union.

    Another preacher, whining, spoke

Of one whose heart for sinners broke;--
He tied old Nanny to an oak,
And drew the blood at every stroke,
And prayed for heavenly union.

Two others oped their iron jaws,
And waved their children-stealing paws;
There sat their children in gewgaws;
By stinting negroes' backs and maws,
They keep up heavenly union.

All good from Jack another takes,
And entertains their flirts and rakes,
Who dress as sleek as glossy snakes,
And cram their mouths with sweetened cakes;
And this goes down for union.

III. SERMON.

BY OLD LORENZO.

> LORD, what is wealth? It will not stay,
> But ever flies away, away,
> As restless waters roll;
> No sort of goods, beyond the grave,
> Will ever meet its owner, save
> A faithful negro's soul.

BRETHREN, did you ever think of the importance of laying up treasures in heaven? What is gold, or houses, or land, or earthly honors? Will they purchase happiness here? Will they secure heaven hereafter? When you "shuffle off this mortal coil," all these things will become as dross, worthless as the sediments of a blacksmith's forge. You tell me, you are going to buy up a store of good works. But what will that avail you. Can you plead your good works at the bar of heaven? Will good works save you? Be not deceived with such a fatal delusion. How are you going to get your good works performed here on earth, to heaven? I tell you, you must have available funds there. They have got a bank up here in the moon. Suppose you could get one of their bills--what would it be worth here? It might be worth something as a curiosity, but as a medium of commerce, it would be worthless as a rag. So of good works; you can't get them to heaven. They are a sort of bank stock, valuable on earth, to be sure, and "nowhere else but there." A draft in heaven, on the Bank of Good Works, located here on earth, would not sell for its cost in white paper. This laying up good works, to purchase an inheritance in heaven, is like bottling jack-o'-lanterns to light up pandemonium.

My hearers, I see you took discouraged. Despair sits brooding on your hearts. "If good works will not save us," I seem to hear you ask, "what will?" Well, I'll tell you:--you must take something that you can get to heaven; that's plain. You must buy niggers. Niggers have souls, and when they die, if they are Orthodox niggers, they go right off to heaven. But, mind you, they must be Orthodox; if they are not, your fat will be in the fire. First, get them converted to the gospel of submission. Preach to them often, from the text "Servants, obey your masters." You will lose nothing by it. If you want to sell them, you can recommend them then, as Christians, and get your money back again; or, if you prefer, you can flog the souls out of them, and lay up a treasure in heaven. Just think of it, Deacon Ashley. Suppose yourself knocking at heaven's gate, and the old turnkey, St. Peter, demanding, "Who comes there?" "Deacon Ashley," you will reply. "What claim do you present to an entrance here?" inquires Peter. Well, now, you see, if you have no claim, you can't get in; so you up and say, "I have property here." "Property here?" asks Peter, in apparent surprise, though I warrant you he knows all about it; "what property?" You will say, "There was my man Cæsar, a member of our church, whom I shot ten years ago, when he attempted to run away. I paid eight hundred dollars for him. I suppose he is here." "Yes," Peter says, "Cæsar is here. Walk in, deacon; where a man's treasure is, there must he be also."

So you see the immense importance of owning slaves. Our hopes of everlasting salvation hang on the institution of slavery; and as McDuffie said, (I think 'twas Mac,) it is the chief corner-stone of our republican edifice. When I look at it in this light, and think of the mad efforts that are now made to abolish this heaven-ordained institution, and thus secure the destruction of the only free government on earth, and the endless misery of all its inhabitants, my very blood boils with horror at sight of an abolitionist. To rob a man of his purse on earth, is inhuman enough; but to rob him of his treasure in heaven is absolutely diabolical. How many millions on millions of dollars have been paid for slaves, who have gone to heaven! So many millions of dollars, of course, laid up as a treasure there. And these fanatics would not only cheat us out of our just rights here, but would plunder us of our treasures in heaven. I am utterly alarmed at the supineness of our church. A few years ago, if an abolitionist attempted to inculcate his abominable doctrines, you stoned him, hissed at him, pelted him with bad eggs, poured water on him with fire engines, and even shot him dead. You then maintained your character as God's church militant. You have now settled down as God's church capitulated. May you buckle on your armor afresh, and, with brickbats and un-merchantable eggs, go forth to defend your treasures in heaven. Amen.

OUR COUNTRYMEN IN CHAINS.

OUR fellow-countrymen in chains,
  Slaves in a land of light and law!
  Slaves crouching on the very plains
  Where rolled the storm of Freedom's war!
  A groan from Eutaw's haunted wood--
  A wail where Camden's martyrs fell--

By every shrine of patriot blood,
From Moultrie's wall and Jasper's well.

By storied hill and hallowed grot,
By mossy wood and marshy glen,
Whence rang of old the rifle-shot,
And hurrying shout of Marion's men!
The groan of breaking hearts is there--
The falling lash-- the fetter's clank!
Slaves--SLAVES are breathing in that air
Which old De Kalb and Sumter drank!

What, ho!--our countrymen in chains!
The whip on WOMAN'S shrinking flesh!

Our soil yet reddening with the stains
Caught from her scourging, warm and fresh!
What! mothers from their children riven!
What! God's own image bought and sold!
AMERICANS to market driven,
And bartered, as the brute, for gold!

Speak! shall their agony of prayer
Come thrilling to our hearts in vain?
To us, whose fathers scorned to bear
The paltry menace of a chain?
To us, whose boast is loud and long
Of holy Liberty and Light--
Say, shall these writhing slaves of wrong
Plead vainly for their plundered Right?

Shall every flap of England's flag
Proclaim that all around are free,
From "farthest Ind" to each blue crag
That beetles o'er the Western Sea?
And shall we scoff at Europe's kings,
When Freedom's fire is dim with us,
And round our country's altar clings
The damning shade of Slavery's curse?

Just God! and shall we calmly rest,
The Christian's scorn--the Heathen's mirth--
Content to live the lingering jest
And by-word of a mocking Earth?
Shall our own glorious land retain
That curse which Europe scorns to bear?
Shall our own brethren drag the chain
Which not e'en Russia's menials wear?

Down let the shrine of Moloch sink,
And leave no traces where it stood;
No longer let its idol drink
His daily cup of human blood:
But rear another altar there,
To Truth, and Love, and Mercy given;
And Freedom's gift, and Freedom's prayer,
Shall call an answer down from Heaven!

J. G. WHITTIER.

www.ingramcontent.com/pod-product-compliance
Lightning Source LLC
Chambersburg PA
CBHW070611170426
43200CB00012B/2655